I0138989

An INTEGRATIVE HABIT *of* MIND

JOHN HENRY NEWMAN
on the Path to Wisdom

FREDERICK D. AQUINO

NIU
PRESS
DeKalb, IL

© 2012 by Northern Illinois University Press

Published by the Northern Illinois University Press, DeKalb, Illinois 60115

All Rights Reserved.

Design by Julia Fauci

Library of Congress Cataloging-in-Publication Data

Aquino, Frederick D., 1963–

An integrative habit of mind: John Henry Newman on the path to wisdom /
Frederick D. Aquino.

p.   cm.

Includes bibliographical references (p.   ) and index.

ISBN 978-0-87580-452-1 (cloth : alk. paper) — ISBN 978-1-60909-053-1 (e-book)

1. Newman, John Henry, 1801–1890. 2. Knowledge, Theory of. 3. Cognition.

4. Education—Philosophy. I. Title.

BX4705.N5A765 2012

230'.2092—dc23

2011045835

For Michelle, David, and Elizabeth

Contents

Acknowledgments

Some of this material has been delivered at Oxford University, The Catholic University of Leuven, The World Universities Forum (Davos, Switzerland), The American Catholic Philosophical Association, Baylor University, The University of Dallas, and McNeese State University. Moreover, some parts of the book are derived from previously published work. Portions of chapter 1 draw from and develop material in my articles, "Thick and Thin: Personal and Communal Dimensions of Communicating Faith," in *Communicating Faith*, ed. John Sullivan (Washington, DC: Catholic University of America Press, 2010), 199–213, and "Broadening Horizons: Constructing an Epistemology of Religious Belief," *Louvain Studies* 30.3 (2005): 198–213. Chapter 2 is a significant revision and expansion of "Externalism and Internalism: A Newman Matter of Proper Fit," *Heythrop Journal* 51 (2010): 1023–1034. I thank the publishers, especially the Trustees for Roman Catholic Purposes Registered and Blackwell Publishing, for permission to use these materials.

Colleagues, students, and friends have read or discussed parts of this book. Over the course of writing and revising this book, I have benefited from the discussions, comments, suggestions, and critical observations of Michelle Aquino, Edward Enright, John Ford, Michael Paul Gallagher, John Groppe, Ben King, Carson Leverett, David Mahfood, Terrence Merrigan, Paul Morris, Derek Neve, John Sullivan, and Adrian Woods. Professors William Abraham of Southern Methodist University and Mark McIntosh of Durham University have offered critical and helpful feedback on the entire manuscript.

I thank my graduate assistants David Mahfood and Carson Leverett for their assistance in finalizing the text. Both offered invaluable editorial insights. I am also grateful to Amy Farranto, Pippa Letsky, and Susan Bean for their help in preparing the manuscript for publication. They have been wonderful and first-rate editors. The book has been improved because of their remarks.

Last, I thank my family—my wife, Michelle; my son, David; and my daughter, Elizabeth—for their patience, support, and love, without which I could not have completed this book and for whom this book is dedicated. They have taught me, in concrete ways, about the importance and challenge of forming an integrative habit of mind.

An Integrative Habit of Mind

INTRODUCTION

"Usually people look at you when they're talking to you. I know that they're working out what I'm thinking, but I can't tell what they're thinking. It is like being in a room with a one-way mirror in a spy film."
—Mark Haddon, *The Curious Incident of the Dog in the Night-Time*

"The goal of philosophy is always the same, to assist men to understand themselves and thus operate in the open, and not wildly, in the dark."
—Isaiah Berlin, *The Power of Ideas*

In this book, my intention is to connect John Henry Newman's thought with recent work in epistemology, philosophy of cognition, and philosophy of education. As I intend to show, an integrative habit of mind—the capacity to see how things fit together in light of one another and how an understanding of this sort relates to the situation at hand—serves as the underlying concept for my approach to and appropriation of particular issues in these areas. In addition, I offer some preliminary suggestions about how the cultivation of an integrative habit of mind shapes the pursuit of wisdom. I say "preliminary" because I do not attempt to flesh out a full-blown theory of wisdom, nor do I try to furnish a comprehensive definition of wisdom. Rather, I unearth and develop themes from select texts in the corpus of Newman's writings and thereby argue that forming, sustaining, and embodying an integrative habit of mind is fundamental to the pursuit of wisdom.

Accordingly, I structure this introduction in the following way. In the first section, I unpack what an integrative habit of mind entails, especially in terms of its intellectual, social, and communal aspects. In the second section, I clarify how select texts in the corpus of Newman's writings figure into the threefold structure of this book (chapters 1–3). In the third section, I explain how the recent discussion about broadening the desiderata (aims, features, and goals) of epistemology informs my rereading of Newman, particularly my emphasis on the evaluative qualities of the cognitive agent. In the fourth section, I provide a brief narrative about recent appropriations of Newman's work and then locate my constructive link between an integrative habit of mind and wisdom within this new line of investigation.

FORMING AN INTEGRATIVE HABIT OF MIND

An integrative habit of mind entails a stable disposition and a capacity to grasp how various pieces of data and areas of inquiry fit together in light of one another, thereby acquiring a more comprehensive understanding of the issue at hand. It also entails deciphering how this kind of understanding applies to a given situation. However, the process of cultivating an integrative habit of mind requires appropriate levels of training, reflection, and the courage to engage and learn from a circle of interlocutors. In other words, people who desire to form an integrative habit of mind engage in practices such as conducting thorough inquiries, carefully scrutinizing evidence and arguments, investigating numerous fields of study, considering alternative explanations, and giving, receiving, and responding to criticism.

Cultivating an integrative habit of mind in fact seldom takes place in isolation. As it happens, the process of forming an integrative habit of mind is profoundly social, communal, and dialogical. The process includes (1) the capacity to draw adeptly from the informed judgments of others, (2) the aptitude to see how the relevant pieces of data cohere, and (3) the ability to discern how the resultant understanding pertains to the context and issues at hand. As I hope to show, however, an integrative habit of mind does not entail an exaggerated claim of autonomy, nor does it involve an unhealthy appeal to authority. Instead, broadening horizons (through critical engagement with others, for example) is indispensable to the processes of seeing how things fit together in light of one another and of learning to render apt judgments in different contexts.

Consequently, the long-standing practice of gleaning insights from others (what contemporary philosophers call epistemic dependence) plays a fundamental role in enabling socially located agents both to move from a particular set of claims to a more comprehensive understanding of the relevant matters at hand and to render well-informed and apt evaluations. As Catherine Elgin points out, our initial judgments "are not comprehensive; they are apt to be jointly untenable; they may fail to serve the purposes to which they are put or to realize the values we want to uphold."[1] Thus, the desire to form, sustain, and embody an integrative habit of mind becomes more evident precisely in the willingness and ability to bring forth one's own views and perspectives before other cognitive agents. Such a commitment includes the readiness to engage others in dialogue with the overall aim of advancing understanding.

The kind of person envisioned here participates in a set of intellectual practices while being surrounded by numerous critics "who stand at different temporal and spatial removes."[2] Reflection done in this way differs from the depiction of a disengaged intellect (or the stance of an epistemic individualist) that claims to rely entirely upon its own judgment of the evidence and not upon the insights of others. As it happens, a network of commitments (philosophical, social, political, religious, moral, etc.) and different social locations (the university, wider society, religious communities, etc.) furnish the "horizons" or contexts within which and from which a person frames problems, makes claims, carefully follows and evaluates alternative points of view, and learns from and responds to the relevant questions and judgments of others.[3] A person, motivated by the desire to cultivate an integrative habit of mind, is integrally bound up with, though not necessarily swallowed up by, a web of interlocutors.[4] The relationship between autonomy and epistemic dependence is complex.

In stressing the interconnected character of forming an integrative habit of mind, I nevertheless retain an emphasis on the individual activities of the cognitive agent. In so doing, I do not collapse the distinction between the activities of the cognitive agent and the relevant people and communities with whom that person interacts.[5] At the same time, the picture of a person assessing evidence and making judgments in isolation from others seems equally problematic and out of touch with what actually happens. The evaluative qualities and properties that we attribute to individuals (understanding, wisdom, and knowledge, for example) are usually "ascribed on grounds that involve an ineliminable reference to factors in the individual subject's social environment."[6]

I therefore recognize, on the one hand, that different commitments and publics overlap in the cognitive agent's desire and capacity to grasp how various pieces of data fit together in light of one another. Accounts that construct neatly defined spaces of reflection and rules of discourse fail to do justice to the actual processes and contexts in which people render judgments about concrete matters. In any case, people who desire to form an integrative habit of mind do not construct "watertight compartments" for isolating claims, commitments, beliefs, and practices.[7] Quite the opposite, they are deeply enmeshed in a set of overlapping practices and contexts, and the resultant expansion of their thinking includes the insights of others.

On the other hand, acknowledging that our starting points are not entirely neutral or completely objective does not suggest that an integrative habit of mind is simply subjective, relativistic, or constrained by community-specific narratives, values, and practices. On the contrary, the process of cultivating an integrative habit of mind calls for the broadening of horizons, and so people, motivated in this way, must be willing to put forth their claims before those who come from radically different perspectives and publics of discourse. A mind-set of this sort requires that we bring our commitments, viewpoints, and arguments before the various ideas and proposals we come across, "working through them, comparing the alternatives they present, with reference to our developing sense of what is important and what we can live with, seeking a fit between experience and conception."[8] Insulating our claims from public scrutiny, then, is foreign to the process of forming an integrative habit of mind; in fact, it cuts against the grain of wisdom. However, not any web of interlocutors will do; the ability to see how things fit together in light of one another is key to the process of deciphering whether what an interlocutor says is worthy of consideration and implementation. The emphasis here is that if a person desires to cultivate an integrative habit of mind, then certainly that person will make evaluations about how to engage various interlocutors.

THE THREEFOLD STRUCTURE OF THE BOOK

Newman, in principle, grounds his theological and philosophical investigations in real-world environments. It is from this methodological commitment, for example, that he seeks to carve out both a fuller account of human cognition and a robust epistemology of religious belief. As I hope to show, however, forming an integrative habit of mind involves something more than an appeal to the actual process of belief-formation. It also calls for the cultivation of relevant evaluative qualities that enable a person to move from a particular to a more comprehensive understanding of the pertinent issues at hand. To proceed in this way does not strip human agents of their thick commitments under the guise of thinly conceived forms of public discourse nor does it insulate these commitments from broader conversations and other perspectives. By "thick" I mean particular practices, beliefs, judgments, and claims that are grounded in a tradition-specific way of thinking and by "thin" I mean a more comprehensive understanding of the issue at hand (or the employment of generally shared principles) that is not strictly reliant upon or reducible to a tradition-specific way of thinking.[9]

With this complex dynamic in mind, I give attention to the question of how the cultivation of an integrative habit of mind shapes the pursuit of wisdom. I draw from some of Newman's writings, though I limit the focus primarily to three works: *Fifteen Sermons Preached before the University of Oxford, An Essay in Aid of a Grammar of Assent,* and *The Idea of a University.* Although the terminology, issues, and contexts are different,[10] all these works, constructively envisioned, share a fundamental concern about forming and training people to cultivate an integrative habit of mind.[11] For example, the brief account of wisdom in the *University Sermons* (Sermon XIV, "Wisdom, as Contrasted with Faith and Bigotry") is conceptually equivalent to a connected view in *The Idea of a University* and the cultivated illative sense in the *Grammar of Assent.* The common aim here is to move from a domain-specific way of thinking to a more comprehensive account of things and to render a synthetic judgment of how things fit together in light of one another. Along these terminological and conceptual lines, Newman does not operate with a discernable distinction between the theoretical and practical dimensions of wisdom. So I will follow in his footsteps.[12] At any rate, the goal is not to work out, in any great detail, the theoretical and practical distinction. As intimated, I am more interested in showing how select features of an integrative habit of mind contribute to the pursuit of wisdom.

Accordingly, this book has a threefold structure. In chapter 1, I argue that an important feature of an integrative habit of mind involves giving greater attention to the conditions (individual, communal, and environmental) under which human cognition actually works and to the role that evaluative qualities play in regulating epistemic conduct. To be more exact, an integrative habit of mind entails broadening horizons. In one sense, the kind of expansion envisioned here involves highlighting the thick aspects of epistemic reflection and conduct. In another sense, the proposal, constructively conceived, calls for a set of intellectual virtues that enables persons (or communities) to engage others from radically different points of view, the result of which is a more comprehensive account of the important issues at hand. An underlying question of chapter 1, then, centers on what kind of evaluative qualities ought to guide the web of interlocutors in a pluralistic setting. The larger challenge involves specifying how such a focus expands human self-understanding.

In chapter 2, I argue that another feature of an integrative habit of mind involves understanding how different aspects of cognitive activity (such as tacit and cultivated forms of judgment) relate to the situation at hand. In this regard, I put Newman's philosophy of cognition—and especially his conception of cultivated judgment (complex assent)—in conversation with recent work on the unreflective and reflective aspects of belief- and judgment-formation. Along these lines, I clarify the extent to which the distinction between the uncultivated and cultivated dimensions of the illative sense in the *Grammar of Assent* relates to the current epistemological discussion about externalism and internalism. However, I shift the focus here to what a distinction of this sort means for developing an account of cultivated judgment (not necessarily what it means for fleshing out an account of justification or knowledge per se). The activity of the uncultivated illative sense is generally equivalent to the process of acquiring rationally acceptable beliefs or making apt judgments, though the cognitive agent is not internally aware of the relevant factors, states, and conditions that justify those beliefs or aptly form those judgments. The cultivated dimension of the illative sense calls for the maturation of cognitive capacities and evaluative qualities, thereby presupposing that some epistemic factors (such as right judgment in reasoning and explaining how things fit together in light of one another) are accessible to a person on this level. Newman's notion of complex assent, as an example of cultivated judgment, stresses the importance of properly directed motivation along with belief-forming processes of acquiring truth, knowledge, understanding, and wisdom. Each modality of the illative sense has a proper place in the noetic structure of human cognition; however, knowing how each modality of human cognition functions in particular situations, as the occasion arises, requires a cultivated judgment of proper fit.

In chapter 3, I argue that an additional feature of an integrative habit of mind involves forming a connected view. More specifically, I argue that a connected view within an educational setting entails grasping how insights from different disciplines fit together in light of one another and showing how this kind of understanding applies to the particular context at hand. However, my proposal recognizes that different conceptions and models of university education exist, and as a result, it does not offer a full-blown vision of education. Following in the steps of Newman (though in a new and different environment), I argue that those charged with teaching and research responsibilities need to pay greater attention to the intellectual formation of persons and not simply to state-of-the-art techniques and learning outcomes. The task at hand focuses on the cultivation of pedagogical and research exemplars, and I hope that such efforts result in a collegial atmosphere of shared understanding and wisdom. An environment of face-to-face interaction helps to foster the pursuit of goals such as truth, knowledge, understanding, and (in the case at hand) wisdom. The interdisciplinarity suggested here is both timely and difficult, and this is precisely the reason that pedagogical and research exemplars are central to the whole enterprise.

A SHIFT IN EMPHASIS

Epistemology, broadly conceived, entails philosophical reflection on particular cognitive aspects and endeavors of human life. The landscape includes—but is not limited to—developing adequate accounts of our cognitive faculties (memory, reason, sense-perception, for example), belief-formation, knowledge, truth, rationality, justification, warrant, understanding, wisdom, the evaluative qualities of cognitive agents (such as the intellectual virtues), and the social dimension of cognitive activities (such as authority, testimony, epistemic evaluation, inquiry).[13] Moreover, the vast range of epistemic ends warrants clarifying what each aspect of cognition constitutes in its own right and perhaps understanding their interrelations (e.g., the relationship between truth and understanding). As a result, a more expansive conception of epistemology recognizes both "a plurality of epistemic values and goals" and diverse strategies for achieving these goals.[14]

The point here is not to determine whether the most appropriate strategy for ordering these goals is epistemic value monism (that is, whether the acquisition of true beliefs is the primary, if not the only, goal, aim, or value of epistemology; whether sense making is the primary, if not the only, goal, aim, or value of epistemology) or epistemic value pluralism (that is, whether truth is one among many other epistemic goals).[15] Rather, the diverse and expansive landscape of contemporary epistemology allows for greater focus on individual goals in their own right as well as on their interrelations. Consequently, the overall aim of this book can be seen as an attempt to decipher what select features of an integrative habit of mind entail, in their own right, and how they contribute to the pursuit of wisdom.

For example, pursuing wisdom is not simply about acquiring true beliefs and avoiding false ones, though such goals are relevant and important in their own right and relate to the issue at hand. No one would deem the phone-book memorizer, who has accumulated true and factual information, a paragon of understanding and wisdom. Conversely, a person with an integrative habit of mind draws insights from a wide range of sources, shows how they fit together in light of one another, and from such an understanding renders apt judgments about concrete matters. This kind of activity is not simply a matter of amassing scraps of knowledge or collecting a bunch of isolated true beliefs. Rather, it entails deciphering a pattern within all the separate bits of information and discerning what is salient in concrete situations.

Recent discussion about broadening the desiderata of epistemology fits nicely into my rereading of Newman. The expansion includes both the features of beliefs (that is, whether a belief is true, justified, an instance of knowledge, coherent, reliably formed, based upon adequate evidence, and whether it has explanatory power) and the evaluative qualities of human agents (that is, whether a person exhibits understanding, wisdom, intellectual honesty, open-mindedness, and tenacity). As Terrence Tilley rightly points out, contemporary philosophical approaches to religion have largely focused on "religious beliefs as properties or dispositions of individuals without regard to their socially embodied religious life."[16] As intimated, my focus on the integrative habit of mind seeks to make sense of the context- and agent-specific aspects of pursuing wisdom.[17] I target the evaluative features of cognitive agents themselves, and as a result I do not restrict the focus to the foundational status of beliefs or to the logical coherence of beliefs.

For this reason, I move in a direction that is different from the standard treatments of Newman, by shifting the focus from properties of beliefs to character traits of human agents. In this regard, most treatments have highlighted Newman's appeal to implicit processes of reasoning and have tried to show how he charted a course between hard rationalism and fideism. Few accounts have offered constructive suggestions as to how Newman's notions of the illative sense in the *Grammar*, of a connected view in *The Idea of a University*, and of wisdom in the *University Sermons* fit together in light of one another—and as to how they play a role in the formation of human agents of wisdom.[18] My constructive proposal of an integrative habit of mind taps precisely into this neglected theme.

An integrative habit of mind certainly allows for diverse styles of epistemic appraisal, especially since these styles seek to obtain different ends. Alvin Goldman, for example, compares in broad terms deontological- and virtue-based approaches to epistemic evaluation. The deontological option sees evaluation primarily as the fulfillment of an epistemic duty, governed by a set of rules and procedures. The key here is that the cognitive agent fulfills the subjective duty to ensure that he or she has justified the relevant beliefs in an epistemically responsible manner.[19] The virtue approach, Goldman argues, stresses the "good-making or bad-making features, relative to some suitable dimensions. In other words, [this approach picks] out certain traits as virtues or vices. The contrast [here] is found among terms of epistemic appraisal."[20] Some people focus on the rules for epistemic appraisal while others stress the intellectual traits of cognitive agents. I intend to show, however, that an integrative habit of mind refuses to pit these styles against each other. For instance, complex assent, as the cultivation of the illative sense, is an obligation for those who are capable of engaging in deliberative and reflective assessment of their beliefs. Newman here spells out specific traits that form the person for such an endeavor.

My focus on the evaluative qualities of cognitive agents, however, is not at the expense of the standard attention given to the properties of beliefs, nor does it replace a traditional approach to belief formation. Newman, for example, is certainly interested in determining whether particular beliefs are rational, true, justified, reliably formed, and based upon adequate evidence. He also envisions human exemplars as fundamental to the transmission and evaluation of beliefs and therefore sees the intellectual formation of such people as an equally important part of what is involved in acquiring wisdom.[21] Accordingly, I change the direction a bit and show how an integrative habit of mind, embedded in Newman's thought, shapes the pursuit of wisdom.

A NEW CONVERSATION?

The project, conceived in this way, seeks to do justice to Newman's writings while drawing some constructive links with contemporary work in the three aforementioned domains. To a certain extent, it moves beyond a purist reading and tries to connect Newman's thought with particular issues in other fields of knowledge. However, a potential dilemma and confusion may emerge. On the one hand, it is clear that Newman operated as a contextual thinker. He generally wrote with a particular context and question in mind. Methodologically speaking, for example, he did not attempt to secure a general theory of knowledge before establishing the extent of one's knowledge that p and understanding of p. As Terrence Merrigan points out, Newman's way of proceeding complicates, prima facie, the search for cohesive or tight systems of thought.[22]

On the other hand, acquiring a coherent account of how various pieces of data fit together in light of one another is fundamental to Newman's conception of a connected view (also described as the enlargement of mind, a philosophical habit of mind, wisdom, and the cultivated form of the illative sense—complex assent). The difference is that such activities begin within a specific context, and the cognitive agent accordingly seeks to move from a particular set of claims to a more comprehensive understanding of the relevant matters at hand.[23] Both the particular and the integrative are fundamental to the pursuit of wisdom—though, as stated earlier, the former is the starting point.

Perhaps a brief narrative will provide some clarification of what I have in mind. I have decided to restrict my remarks to some recent philosophical and theological appropriations of Newman precisely because such a focus makes the most logical sense in terms of my stated goal of showing how the cultivation of an integrative habit of mind shapes the pursuit of wisdom. However, I recognize that the various stages in Newman studies are important in their own right, and this is neither the time nor the place to map out a formal list of all the possible options. Nevertheless, the scholarly interest—from different philosophical and theological perspectives—in the constructive possibilities of Newman's thought merits attention. An emphasis of this sort differs from the largely historical and descriptive treatments of Newman's thought. However, the attempt to extend his thought into new territory clearly risks taking some mistaken hermeneutical turns and, as noted, risks being perceived as out of touch with both Newman and our contemporary context.

Two points seem relevant. First, the contemporary reader should not expect Newman, a nineteenth-century thinker, to come with a corpus of ready-made answers to our contemporary questions, concerns, and hermeneutical inquiries.[24] Rather, the ongoing task is to decipher possible connections, working through the subtleties of Newman's own proposal while engaging in rigorous constructive work. Second, holding Newman captive to his own context renders constructive possibilities nearly impossible. This hermeneutical conundrum is not unique to the ongoing task of rethinking Newman's relevance for today; it comes with the territory of unearthing and unpacking themes and proposals in any figure of significance. The key to connecting Newman's thought with our own context is a balance of analytical precision and constructive vision.

A constructive emphasis, however, finds some resistance beyond purist demands; it also comes in the form of philosophical criticism. For some time, the philosophical side of Newman's work has been largely ignored,[25] underestimated,[26] and written off as so problematic as to question the possibility of any constructive promise, at least in the philosophical arena. For example, some have claimed that the *Grammar of Assent* fits the description of a phenomenology of religious belief with no authentic traces of epistemic reflection. In other words, Newman's preference for a strong phenomenological basis creates a deep chasm between psychological and epistemic conditions of belief- and agent-formation.

Such an impression, as I intend to show, is misleading, especially since Newman maps out (in the *Grammar*) a proposal about how inquiries (about religious belief, for example) ought to be regulated, and not simply about how the process of belief formation in fact occurs. It is true that the personal nature of the illative sense of reasoning, as developed in the *Grammar*, complicates the search for a common ground by which radically different communities can adjudicate truth claims. Newman's own recognition of the problem of common measure—the problem of adjudicating radically different claims through an appeal to the personal dimension of the illative—leads some to categorize him as a skeptic, a fideist, a subjectivist, and a relativist.

A new line of investigation of Newman's philosophical thought has emerged within the last 40 or 50 years. This level of interest may parallel the expansion of topics and areas of exploration within the analytical stream of philosophy. For example, some have recently placed Newman's focus on the illative sense within the naturalist tradition and the more recent manifestation of naturalized epistemology, thereby rethinking the connection between psychological and epistemic conditions of belief formation.[27] Others have shown how the contemporary strategies of reliabilism, virtue epistemology, and social epistemology unearth and develop the epistemic insights in Newman's notion of the illative sense and perhaps help address the problem of the common measure and the charges of fideism, relativism, and skepticism.[28]

Why have these aspects of Newman's thought been overlooked for so long? Perhaps the prominence of his work in the areas of education, doctrinal development, lay involvement in the church, and spiritual autobiography has contributed to this philosophical oversight. Certainly, Newman's posture as a contextual thinker may cause some to disqualify him from wearing the titles of philosopher and theologian, given that his methodological commitments do not fit the so-called standard expectations of how philosophers and theologians ought to proceed. However, recent treatments have shown how Newman, at least methodologically speaking, is a logical extension of (though not reducible to) the naturalist tradition and the particularistic slant of epistemology. The expanded territory of contemporary epistemology and the concomitant expansion of desiderata have certainly made such connections possible and have made it more difficult to exclude Newman from the enterprises of philosophy and theology.

Another explanation may be that some have tried to capture Newman's thought in one trajectory, school of thought, and tradition. However, his thought is profoundly dynamic, multifaceted, contextual, integrative, and existential. The failure to discern the complexity of his appropriation of diverse resources perhaps explains why people from various perspectives employ him to support their positions and polarize the theological landscape. As Merrigan points out, Newman's "ability to hold in tensile unity apparently opposite tendencies and concerns" comes with the territory of being a thinker grounded in a real-world environment. In addition, Merrigan aptly summarizes the hermeneutical problem, especially as it relates to the elasticity, complexity, and varied reception of Newman's thought. Indeed, one of the most revealing signs is the extent to which the corpus of Newman's writings has been appropriated by "nearly every shade of theological opinion. So-called conservative no less than so-called progressive Catholics can find in Newman's writings remarks that appear to serve their particular theological agendas."[29]

On a more positive note, the complexity of Newman's thought and the resultant history of interpretation can be evidenced in recent interpretations, either as full treatments of his thought or as a part of a larger project. For instance, Basil Mitchell,[30] Jamie Ferreira,[31] William Wainwright,[32] Joseph Dunne,[33] Martin Moleski,[34] William Abraham,[35] Frederick Aquino,[36] Mark Wynn,[37] Thomas Carr,[38] and others have all worked through Newman's thought, trying to show how his particular conceptual moves fit contemporary issues in philosophy of religion, philosophy of education, philosophical theology, systematic theology, and religious epistemology. Such works have gleaned insights, though not in purist terms, from the corpus of Newman's writings. They have tried to form constructive links with contemporary issues such as an informal cumulative case for theism (Mitchell), the importance of a properly disposed heart for evaluating evidence (Wainwright, Wynn), the retrieval of Aristotelian phronesis in light of modern rationalism (Dunne), a post-critical theology of personal knowledge (Moleski), an epistemology of divine revelation through the notion of threshold (Abraham), a religious philosophy of aesthetics (Carr), Newman in the context of the naturalist tradition (Ferreira), and an account of informed judgment in conversation with social and virtue epistemologies (Aquino).

Newman's thought seems to be finding new homes, sometimes in places least expected. In fact, exploring this varied landscape may have more promise than in some easily anticipated areas. Wisdom does not back off from truth claims, but neither does it ignore the challenge of seeing how things fit together from various resources, traditions, and people. I hope the conversation expands, and the desire to link Newman's thought with different fields of knowledge becomes a collaborative effort. Cultivating an integrative habit of mind is precisely what I want to emphasize in this book. Along these lines, I hope to show how the pursuit of wisdom—informed by Newman's thought—is relevant to our contemporary context.

——— *Chapter One* ———

BROADENING HORIZONS

"We see but in part, and we know but in part, and therefore it is no wonder we conclude not right from our partial views. This might instruct the proudest esteemer of his own parts, how useful it is to talk and consult with others, even such as came short of him in capacity, quickness and penetration: for since no one sees all, and we generally have different prospects of the same thing, according to our different, as I may say, positions to it, it is not incongruous to think nor beneath any man to try whether another may not have notions of things which have escaped him, and which his reason would make use of if they came into his mind."

—John Locke, *Of the Conduct of the Understanding*

An important feature of an integrative habit of mind entails giving greater attention to the conditions (individual, communal, and environmental) under which human cognition actually works and to the role that evaluative qualities play in regulating epistemic reflection and conduct. A focus of this sort opens up new possibilities for exploring how processes and practices of intellectual formation enable the cognitive agent both to move from a particular set of claims to a more comprehensive understanding of the relevant issues at hand and to expand intellectual horizons. Broadening horizons in one sense involves highlighting the thick aspects of epistemic reflection and conduct. In another sense, it calls for a set of intellectual virtues that enables persons or communities both to engage others from radically different points of view and to acquire a more comprehensive account of the important issues at hand.

I will flesh out Newman's overall argument for a thicker yet richer conception of epistemic reflection and conduct. Then I will offer some suggestions as to what a proposal of this sort means for the pursuit of wisdom. Included here is a discussion of how a sacramental way of thinking captures the intersection of rigorous reflection and a religious way of being in the world. I will unpack the challenge of navigating epistemic reflection and conduct in a context where people come from radically different perspectives and commitments. I argue that finding viable ways of connecting thick and thin commitments is fundamental to taking up the task of forming an integrative habit of mind. Within a pluralistic context of this sort, a robust account of an integrative habit of mind (instantiated as an embodied particularism of informed judgment) includes the cultivation of intellectual virtues as indispensable for guiding the process of intellectual exchange.

MOVE TO THE CONCRETE

In a letter to Father Walford, Newman describes the *Grammar of Assent* as "a conversational essay" and not "a didactic treatise." It is "a preliminary opening of the ground."[1] In another letter, Newman acknowledges that this work "may be full of defects, and certainly characterized by incompleteness and crudeness, but it is something to have started a problem, and mapped in part a country, if I have done nothing more."[2] Thinking of the *Grammar* in this way conveys at least two impressions. On the one hand, Newman does not consider its arguments and conclusions to be comprehensive, definitive, or final. After all, the full title of the book is *An Essay in Aid of a Grammar of Assent*, so it seems appropriate to regard the work as a conversational piece or as a preliminary investigation. On the other hand, the structure, arguments, and content of the *Grammar* call for a closer look at the actual processes of belief- and agent-formation. Although the *Grammar* fleshes out the conditions under which a religious belief—along with other beliefs (such as belief in the existence of the external world)—is phenomenologically and epistemically rational, it also maps out a proposal about how inquiries ought to be conducted.

Along these lines, on the title page of the *Grammar* Newman includes a quotation from Ambrose's *De Fide ad Gratianum Augustum*: "Non in dialectica complacuit Deo salvum facere populum suum" (It did not please God to save his people by means of logic). The *Grammar* is not, technically speaking, an exegesis of *De Fide ad Gratianum Augustum*.[3] Rather, the Ambrosian line captures a pervasive theme in Newman's thinking about the nature and scope of human cognition, namely, a shift of emphasis from "paper logic" (human cognition reduced to formal logical arguments on paper) to how human cognition actually works in real-world environments.[4] Thus, the correlative relevance of the Ambrosian line actually lies in carving out a fuller account of belief- and agent-formation.

Rereading Ambrose in this way, however, does not suggest a flat-out rejection of logic. Instead, Newman wants to show that the scope, range, and modalities of human cognition cover more territory than an ideal version of rationality (an explicit kind of reasoning, for example).[5] In this regard, a basic claim in the *Grammar* is that "truth sinks slowly into the mind, and that therefore paper argument is most disappointing."[6] As a result, Newman's proposal calls for a fuller account of belief formation that includes automatic and deliberative aspects of human cognition and envisions intellectual formation as the integration of the cognitive, affective, and volitional facets of the self.[7]

The *Grammar* also depicts intellectual formation as something more than following a rule-governed process. Practice and experience are crucial for reasoning well and making apt judgments in concrete situations. Though not with Newman in mind, Martha Nussbaum sheds light on what is entailed in learning to render apt judgments in different contexts:

> For teaching and learning, here, do not simply involve the learning of rules and principles. A large part of learning takes place in the experience of the concrete. This experiential learning, in turn, requires the cultivation of perception and responsiveness: the ability to read a situation, singling out what is relevant for thought and action. This active task is not a technique; one learns it by guidance rather than by a formula.[8]

Newman's notion of the illative sense comes close to this description. An emphasis on broadening horizons coheres, to some extent, with recent work on the non-reflective and reflective aspects of belief- and judgment-formation.

Appealing to the Ambrosian line makes sense, especially in a context where some gravitate toward reductionistic accounts of rationality. Consider, for example, the evidentialism of Newman's day. The basic claim of this version of evidentialism is that one is rationally entitled to believe that p, if and only if one possesses full understanding of p and demonstrative proof of p.[9] Religious beliefs that fail to meet these criteria are simply matters of opinion and sentiment. If one cannot render sufficient reasons for believing that p, one is not entitled to claim p as rationally acceptable. Thus, one is epistemically obligated to reject "every thing but the actual evidence producible in its favour" (*US* 188) of p. To do otherwise is to commit an intellectual vice or shirk one's intellectual duty and, therefore, to be epistemically irresponsible and negligent.

Newman's earlier experiences in the circle of the Oriel Noetics furnish a nice glance into commitments of this sort. The Noetics sought to put forth formal arguments for Christian belief on paper. For example, Richard Whately, a prominent member of the Noetics, argues that the cultivation of "*argumentative powers*" is indispensable for defending the Christian faith. A person "desirous of possessing a cultivated mind" must master formal logic, the science of reasoning.[10] All reasoning, Whately adds, "on whatever subject, is one and the same process, which may be clearly exhibited in the form of Syllogisms" (*EL* 253, see also 258, 262).[11] Consequently, the Noetics mirrored the evidentialism of the day and reduced Christian belief "to little more than logical deduction from certain evidences for the divine character of Christianity."[12] There is little room for including mystery and, more specifically, for considering the role of the implicit and the tacit in the process of belief formation.[13]

Although he shares the concern for providing an intellectual account of religious belief, Newman views the Noetic commitment as phenomenologically problematic and epistemically narrow. The Noetics fail to ground their insights in the actual processes of belief- and judgment-formation and in the domain-specific contexts of reasoning. Nevertheless, Newman acknowledges and appreciates the impact of the Noetics on his own thinking, especially Whately's guidance on the requisite habits for regulating epistemic reflection and conduct.[14] As Newman notes, Whately, "emphatically, opened my mind, and taught me to think and use my reason . . . he had not only taught me to think, but to think for myself" (*Apo* 22).[15] In addition, Newman helped Whately write the *Elements of Logic* in the summer of 1822. This kind of opportunity gave Newman a firsthand glance into the history of logic and its significance for belief formation.[16]

Newman's criticism of the Noetics, then, is not directed at the demand for intellectual rigor and logical precision, nor is it aimed at the attempt to furnish guidelines for assessing evidence. Rather, Newman's disagreement is over the Noetic assumption about the nature, function, and scope of human cognition, especially in terms of forming and sustaining religious beliefs. In the *Elements of Logic*, Whately acknowledges that simple apprehension, judgment, and reasoning are three operations of the mind. However, the third operation alone is the "appropriate province" of logic, and "the rest being treated of only in reference to that" (*EL* 172). Accordingly, the primary business of logic "is with *argumentation*, expressed in words, and the operations of the mind implied in that: what others there may be, or whether any are irrelevant questions" (*EL* 60).

Newman identifies this mode of reasoning in the *University Sermons* as explicit reasoning and in the *Grammar* as formal inference.[17] Skill in formal logical thinking, though helpful and appropriate in its own right, does not fully capture all that goes into identifying salient facts and features in concrete situations. A fuller account of belief formation accordingly includes "an *organon* more delicate, versatile, and elastic than verbal argumentation" (*GA* 217). The scope of human cognition, in other words, is not restricted to explicit or formal thinking. Some people, for example, proceed "by a sort of instinctive perception of the legitimate conclusion in and through the premises, not by a formal juxtaposition of propositions" (*GA* 239).

The Noetic abstractions thin out the concrete aspects of cognitive activities, debilitate the confidence of most ordinary believers, and contribute to a growing yet artificial chasm between faith and reason. Conversely, Newman's transformation in thinking reflects a desire to spell out an alternative account. As a result, the Ambrosian line sums up the deep impression that the patristic conception of personal and concrete reasoning had on Newman's understanding of belief formation and of epistemic reflection. In the *Apologia*, for example, Newman offers a brief commentary on the relevance of the Ambrosian line:

> And then I felt altogether the force of the maxim of St. Ambrose, "Non in dialectica complacuit Deo salvum facere populum suum;"—I had a great dislike of paper logic. For myself, it was not logic that carried me on; as well

might one say that the quicksilver in the barometer changes the weather. It is the concrete being that reasons; pass a number of years, and I find my mind in a new place; how? The whole man moves; paper logic is but the record of it. All the logic in the world would not have made me move faster towards Rome than I did; as well might you say that I have arrived at the end of my journey, because I see the village church before me, as venture to assert that the miles, over which my soul had to pass before it got to Rome, could be annihilated, even though I had been in possession of some far clearer view than I then had, that Rome was my ultimate destination. . . . And a greater trouble still than these logical mazes, was the introduction of logic into every subject whatever, so far, that is, as this was done. Before I was at Oriel, I recollect an acquaintance saying to me that the "Oriel Common Room stank of Logic." One is not at all pleased when poetry, or eloquence, or devotion, is considered as if chiefly intended to feed syllogisms. (*Apo* 136)

Again, this observation does not imply a rejection of logic; it simply clarifies the difference between reaching "a conclusion in the abstract" and coming to "a conclusion in the concrete" (*Apo* 136). Newman thinks that logic plays an important role in evaluating beliefs and navigating epistemic conduct—as his notions of complex assent (a person knows that he or she knows *p*) in the *Grammar* and of a connected view (discerning how various ideas hang together in light of one another) in *The Idea of a University* attest. Nonetheless, he also stresses the personal and social conditions of belief formation. So his criticism is against the assumption that one is rationally entitled to believe that *p*, if and only if one possesses full understanding and demonstrative proof of *p*.

Newman's approach to belief- and agent-formation recognizes the historical, social, and developmental aspects of thought and the extent to which people come to evidence from different intellectual standpoints (such as first principles, training, experience). The illative sense, for example, reflects the personal dimension in judging the validity of claims. Its activity "economizes to [the] subject matter with deliberation moving back and forth dialectically," adjusting "in relation to the whole person within the community of discourse as the context within which thought develops progressively."[18] Newman, like Aristotle, sees "fine-tuned *concreteness*"[19] as an indispensable ingredient for making informed judgments, especially since "it is the concrete being that reasons" (*Apo* 136).[20] The exercise of the illative sense, which is analogous to the formation of good judgment in the area of morality (e.g., Aristotle's notion of *phronesis*—practical wisdom), also depends on the level of sagacity, skill, or prudence cultivated by a person (*GA* 280). Practice and experience are crucial for reasoning well and making apt judgments in concrete situations. Deciphering the activity of the illative sense is a matter of proper fit. However, the notion of proper fit does not suggest that Newman is a radical subjectivist. Although he believes that humans are wired for acquiring truth, Newman acknowledges that the route is complicated and therefore intellectual formation is warranted.

This kind of approach to belief- and agent-formation highlights both concrete and integrative aspects of epistemic reflection and conduct. In using the word "concrete," I draw attention to the actual contexts in which people form beliefs (that is, how cognition actually works) and cultivate evaluative qualities (that is, the role that intellectual virtues play in regulating how people ought to conduct themselves epistemically).[21] The cultivation of evaluative qualities is more relevant to the task at hand. In using the word "integrative," I stress the importance of moving from a particular set of claims to a connected view of things. A connected view of things in teachers and researchers (that is, grasping how insights from different disciplines fit together in light of one another and showing how this kind of understanding applies to the context at hand) is a crucial feature of an integrative habit of mind and is equally relevant for the contemporary scene (as I hope to show below, in chapter 3).

Ultimately, a shift from "paper logic" to how human cognition works in real-world environments challenges the claim that complex operations of the mind can be summed up on paper or that verbal skills of argumentation exhaust the operation of the mind.[22] It begins with a focus on environmental and person-specific conditions, followed by an exploration of how a particular set of claims can be expanded to a more comprehensive understanding of things. In the *University Sermons*, the *Grammar of Assent*, and the *Idea of a University*, for example, Newman grounds the processes of religious belief—such as faith and reason as habits of mind, implicit and explicit modalities of reasoning, and simple and complex assents—and of intellectual formation (such as wisdom, a connected view, and the cultivation of the illative sense) in the concrete and broader contours of human experience. These processes are certainly subject to rigorous philosophical reflection, but critical assessment of this sort must take into account the ways that built-in cognitive capacities (visual processing, for example), experience, tradition, and dependence on the insights of others contribute to belief formation and epistemic conduct.[23]

ON THE PATH TO WISDOM—
FROM A SACRAMENTAL ANGLE

Focusing on the context- and agent-specific aspects of pursuing wisdom in this way is clearly the work of a person encircled by different interlocutors from both the past and the present. For instance, Newman's account of belief- and agent-formation draws insights—though not uncritically—from both ancient and modern writers (that is, the sacramental principle articulated by Clement of Alexandria and Origen, the personal reasoning of patristic writers such as Ambrose, the Aristotelian tradition of *phronesis*, the naturalist tradition of Locke and Hume, and Butler's argument from probability). The capacity to appropriate insights from different thinkers—and sometimes from conflicting commitments—complicates attempts to attach Newman's line of argumentation to a single school of thought.

Moreover, avenues for pursuing wisdom are varied. As a result, recognizing the difference between ontological realities and philosophical strategies is crucial to the process of seeking wisdom.[24] This kind of distinction, for Newman, can be traced back to the sacramental principle articulated by Clement of Alexandria and Origen:

> The broad philosophy of Clement and Origin carried me away; the philosophy, not the theological doctrine; and I have drawn out some features of it in my volume, and with the zeal and freshness, but with the partiality, of a neophyte. Some portions of their teaching, magnificent in themselves, came like music to my inward ear, as if the response to ideas, which, with little external to encourage them, I had cherished so long. These were based on the mystical or sacramental principle, and spoke of the various Economies or Dispensations of the Eternal. I understood these passages [in Clement of Alexandria and Origen] to mean that the exterior world, physical and historical, was but the manifestation to our senses of realities greater than itself. Nature was a parable. . . . The visible world still remains without its divine interpretation; Holy Church in her sacraments and her hierarchical appointments, will remain, even to the end of the world, after all but a symbol of

those heavenly facts which fill eternity. Her mysteries are but the expressions
in human language of truths to which the human mind is unequal. (*Apo* 34)

From a sacramental angle, cognitive agents in trying to make sense of
divine matters understand the material world as fundamentally connected to but not equivalent to reality.[25] Thus, a person who embodies
a sacramental way of thinking probes the deeper mysteries of faith,
thereby seeking to expand horizons through fuller and richer aspects of
epistemic reflection and conduct.

Instead of positing a God's-eye point of view, the preliminary emphasis here is on the actual conditions under which cognitive agents move
from a particular grasp of things to a more comprehensive vision. For
this reason, Newman rejects the Cartesian claim that we "ought to begin
with universal doubt." Global skepticism of this sort "is of all assumptions the greatest, and to forbid assumptions universally is to forbid this
one in particular. Doubt itself is a positive state, and implies a definite
habit of mind, and thereby necessarily involves a system of principles
and doctrines all its own" (*GA* 294).

Newman opts for what contemporary philosophers call the principle
of credulity. It is prima facie reasonable "that we ought to begin with
believing everything that is offered to our acceptance," unless we have
specific reasons to believe otherwise. If we discover errors along the way
in our thinking, we discard them and modify our claims (*GA* 294).[26] For
example, a person may have undefeated experiential evidence for the
claim that there is a mesquite tree in front of him or her but could still
lack a definitive argument for this claim. In this example, the person is
prima facie justified in believing in p (that is, relying on one's perceptual experience) without satisfying a rigorous philosophical standard
of adjudication. Nevertheless, Newman recognizes the importance of
critically assessing beliefs—though not with a Cartesian requirement as
a starting point. As a result, the principle of credulity does not insulate
one's perspective from critical examination, nor does it ignore the question about the adequate grounds upon which one's beliefs are based.

Thickening epistemic reflection and conduct in this way certainly complicates the goal of achieving a "common measure" among people from
different perspectives (*GA* 82–83). Securing an independent standard of
justification seems deeply problematic, especially given the reality that
interpretive disagreements stem from different levels of training and the

employment of different first principles. Awareness of the problematic nature of finding an independent standard of justification is precisely the reason that cognitive agents, guided by the integrative habit of mind, must stretch out their epistemic necks, engage in intellectual exchange with others, and seek to see how various pieces of data fit together in light of one another. In this regard, a theologically and philosophically mature mind results from interacting with others despite the difficulty of adjudicating claims from different perspectives and sources.[27]

A sacramental way of thinking includes apophatic and cataphatic elements, thereby guarding against intellectual vices such as superstition, dogmatism, and fanaticism:[28]

> We can do no more than put ourselves on the guard as to our own proceeding, and protest against it, while we do [adhere to] it. We can only set right one error of expression by another. By this method of antagonism we steady our minds, not so as to reach their object, but to point them in the right direction; as in an algebraic process we might add and subtract in series, approximating little by little, by saying and unsaying, to a positive result . . . [God] is ineffably one yet [God] is exuberantly manifold.[29]

The dialectic of affirmation and negation furnishes a safeguard against conflating epistemic attempts to make sense of reality with reality itself. However, recognizing the limitations of human discourse about God does not warrant flimsy thinking, nor does it sanction a retreat from dealing with intellectual difficulties.[30] Instead, acknowledging the mysteries of faith means acquiring greater appreciation for the expansive nature of religious reflection, thereby exhibiting the kind of intellectual honesty that realizes complexities surrounding particular beliefs.

By way of caveat, a proposal of this sort coheres with current interest in seeing how patristic insights inform the task of theology.[31] In terms of cultivating an integrative habit of mind, theology seeks to graft the whole person into the complex process of seeking knowledge, understanding, and wisdom of divine matters and of being changed by them. However, theology envisioned in this way does not exclude the study of logic, history, science, and other fields of knowledge. Rather, it deciphers how such endeavors contribute to the more comprehensive task of forming people of intellectual excellence. Contemplation and rigorous reflection, for example, are complementary practices that mold the pursuit of wisdom.

Theology, after all, is a contextual enterprise, a vibrant pursuit of a living mind saturated in the concrete moments of human existence. It is not "a fixed and static teaching systematically imposed irrespective of times and circumstances, but it originated in living and fundamentally imaginative response to the mysteries of revealed truth; what had to keep on changing, if it were to live was our understanding of it."[32] The theologian, like the philosopher, employs discourse that shapes the formation of cognitive agents. The goal is not to convey "some ready-made knowledge but to *form*" people through intellectual, moral, and spiritual exercises. The result is the development of "a *habitus*, or new capacity to judge and to criticize; and to *transform*—that is, to change people's way of living and seeing the world."[33] Newman calls such activity (the ability to make salient connections and apply these insights to concrete situations) wisdom in the *University Sermons*, the cultivated illative sense in the *Grammar*, and a connected view in *The Idea of a University.*[34]

With this in mind, an integrative habit of mind seeks to bridge the chasm between epistemic reflection (reasoning well, understanding how things follow, and how they fit together in light of one another) and a concrete way of being in the world (the kind of life that one's philosophical and theological commitments imagine and inhabit) without blurring this fundamental distinction. Connecting discourse and way of life has a contemporary parallel in the work of the French philosopher Pierre Hadot. Early in his intellectual training, Hadot credits Newman for this insight:

> Newman shows in this work [the *Grammar*] that it's not the same thing to give one's assent to an affirmation which one understands in a purely abstract way, and to give one's assent while engaging one's entire being, and 'realizing'—in the English sense of the word—with one's heart and one's imagination, just what this affirmation means for us. This distinction between real and notional assent underlies my research on spiritual exercises. . . . Ever since I started doing philosophy, I've always believed that philosophy was a concrete act, which changed our perception of the world, and our life: not the construction of a system. It is life, not a discourse.[35]

Hadot's preference for the concrete is similar to Newman's kind of particularism. Thus, both moving from thick commitments to a more comprehensive understanding of the relevant matters at hand and embodying a more holistic way of being in the world are fundamental to the formation of an integrative habit of mind.

Justification for the appeal to ancient Greek and patristic understand-ings of philosophy is not self-evident in most contemporary circles. The focus on a philosophical way of life is foreign to most current approaches to philosophy; rather, the primary concern is the theoretical undertak-ing of conceptual issues. The contemporary philosopher Michael Wil-liams aptly notes the difference between ancient and contemporary approaches to epistemic reflection:

> Ancient philosophy, it has been plausibly argued, is practical through and through. For the ancients, philosophy is at bottom a certain way of life.... On this account, ancient philosophy is not what philosophy is today: a primar-ily (or even exclusively) theoretical undertaking. The ancient understanding of philosophy still echoes strongly in the popular conception of the subject and often causes embarrassment to professional philosophers when they find themselves in conversation with the laity, who are disappointed to find that professional philosophers are not always outstandingly wise or even full of advice.[36]

Nussbaum sees a similar eclipse of the transformative aspect of philo-sophical reflection:

> Most professional philosophers did not, I found, share the ancient concep-tion of philosophy as discourse addressed to nonexpert readers of many kinds who would bring to the text their urgent concerns, questions, needs, and whose souls might in that interaction be changed. Having lost that con-ception they had lost, too, the sense of the philosophical text as an expressive creation whose form should be part and parcel of its conception, revealing in the shape of the sentences the lineaments of a human personality with a particular sense of life.[37]

To some extent, Newman's project resembles the ancient emphasis on the link between reflection and way of life. However, his focus on how people reason within real-world environments (that is, the context- and agent-specific aspects of epistemic reflection and conduct) and on form-ing an integrative aspect of epistemic reflection puts him in ancient and modern company (with Aristotle, John Locke, Joseph Butler, Thomas Reid, Abraham Tucker, Joshua Reynolds, and David Hume, for example).

Newman's retrieval of the context- and agent-specific aspects of hu-man cognition in the ancient Greek and patristic traditions does not downgrade the theoretical component, nor does it ignore the ongoing task of achieving a connected view. Rather, an important part of broadening horizons involves taking into account the subjective and objective conditions under which an integrative habit of mind is formed.[38] In this regard, the tendency to reduce religious belief to either domain is analogous to contemporary attempts to dissolve the gap between first-person and third-person experiences. For example, observing human behavior or the function of the brain does not give us full access to first-person experiences or explain how physical processes give rise to a rich inner life. We also know that the path of folk psychology is plagued with the problem of credulity. The call to consider various insights will be painful but necessary to our quest for a richer conception of epistemic reflection and conduct. We have a long journey ahead of us as we try to foster a conversation between the scientific image and the humanist vision of things. An integrative habit of mind is especially needed for working through these challenges.

Consequently, an integrative habit of mind takes into account the complex dynamic between implicit and explicit processes of belief- and agent-formation. The aim here is to understand afresh how intellectual practices contribute to the acquisition of an integrative habit of mind and (more importantly) shape the pursuit of wisdom. Thus, an alternative to the divorce between spirituality and philosophical reflection (e.g., epistemology) is an integrative approach that sees these domains of inquiry as sacramental mediations.

To move in this constructive direction, we must be prepared for painful seasons of existence, shedding the old habits of reductionism and sentimentality, and so forth. For example, the pursuit of wisdom, sacramentally envisioned through the lens of an integrative habit of mind, rethinks the connection between religious and other forms of inquiry.[39] The aim here is to reflect on and decipher how insights from various fields of knowledge (biology, psychology, history, philosophy, and so on) hang together in light of one another. Newman, as we have seen, understands the material world as fundamentally connected to but not equivalent to reality.

This sacramental principle is deeply particularistic and integrative, keenly focusing on the historical, social, personal, religious, and philosophical dimensions of human selfhood. An emphasis of this sort targets the actual conditions of how cognitive agents are and ought to be formed and, in so doing, shapes my constructive focus on the pursuit of wisdom.

We are "faced all the time with new and complex situations; how we deal with them reveals what we have become and affects what we are becoming."[40] Forming an integrative habit of mind calls for constructive and imaginative possibilities mediated through cognitive agents, struggling to connect discourse and way of life. A sacramental way of proceeding, then, is an extension of the Ambrosian move from paper logic to how human cognition actually works in real-world environments. From a sacramental angle, an integrative habit of mind involves making sense of divine matters and understanding the material world and cognitive activities as fundamentally connected to but not equivalent to reality.

THE PROBLEM OF PARTICULARITY

Stressing a thicker construal of epistemic reflection and conduct will inevitably give rise to profound levels of anxiety. A problem of this sort stems from a persistent concern over how to handle intellectual challenges, conceptual differences, and varied kinds of cognitive dissonance. By now, most of us have tried different philosophical therapies to heal the intellectual wounds of our past. Yet we continue to participate in and feel the impact of a long-standing crisis of authority (both religious and nonreligious) in our current settings, and the wounds remain open. The effects of the crisis are evident in our struggle to navigate a sustainable intellectual path, in the hope of securing some epistemic closure or at least finding an appropriate salve to relieve the pain.

With these challenges in mind, how does one engage in the ongoing task of forming an integrative habit of mind? What links people from radically different starting points and commitments? Newman failed to resolve the problem (for example in the *Grammar*) of how an emphasis on the context- and agent-specific aspects of the illative sense secures a common measure among different minds.[41] My interest is both to unearth and develop themes from select texts in the corpus of Newman's writings and to argue that forming, sustaining, and embodying an integrative habit of mind is fundamental to the pursuit of wisdom. However, my intention is not to rehearse Newman's basic moves. Rather, I recognize the promise of Newman's approach to belief- and agent-formation while acknowledging the limits of his thought within its own context.

In this section, I unpack the crisis of authority briefly and then, in the next section, show how an integrative habit of mind—materialized as an embodied particularism of informed judgment—takes up these challenges and questions. This kind of particularism has a synthetic component, in that cognitive agents draw insights from an expansive range of sources and therefore are able to move from the particular to the more comprehensive. A proposal of this sort challenges accounts that insulate thick commitments (e.g., tradition-specific ways of thinking) from broader conversations or those that strip cognitive agents of their particular habits, practices, and beliefs under the guise of thinly conceived forms of public discourse. Conversely, informed judgment calls for a richer conception of intellectual formation that includes rigorous communicative, philosophical, moral, and religious practices.

But how do people navigate the discourse when thick and thin commitments seem incommensurable? One can see the impact of this kind of quandary on contemporary debates concerning theories of knowledge, truth, rationality, warrant, consciousness, human selfhood, meaning, value, and perception. The failure to agree on the locus of authority for judging religious and nonreligious issues has certainly intensified, and continues to fuel the long search for new grounds of epistemic certainty. The broader publics today very much recognize the crisis. A current example is the hot topic of religion's role in the public and, more specifically, the question of whether religion is detrimental to human flourishing.[42] The list of issues is extensive.

The epistemic anxiety thus described gives rise to different responses. I mention two general tendencies. One option is the attempt to transcend the contingencies of history and tradition, thereby removing the shackles of ignorance, wish fulfillment, and outdated cosmologies. The goal is to identify hindrances steeped in the particular and move toward a thinner mode of discourse. Reason, experience, and education are some of the candidates for purging and healing cognitive impurities. An aim of this kind is admirable, noble, and relevant, yet proponents of such projects occasionally receive a grave reminder of the human potential to engage in dehumanizing activities. In this regard, Jonathan Glover masterfully captures the tension between the human quest for enlightenment and the human potential for the tragic:

> At the start of the century there was optimism, coming from the Enlightenment, that the spread of a humane and scientific outlook would lead to the fading away, not only of war, but also of other forms of cruelty and

barbarism. They would fill the chamber of horrors in the museum of our primitive past. In the light of these expectations, the century of Hitler, Stalin, Pol Pot and Saddam Hussein was likely to be a surprise. Volcanoes thought extinct turned out not to be.[43]

My point here is not to belittle the Enlightenment project (a popular move) but simply to underscore the humane and inhumane facets of such an effort and to remind us of the lingering effects of the epistemic crisis.

Another option is the full embrace of irony, contingency, and play. A hermeneutical posture of this sort constitutes a radical move toward the thick (the particular). The inclination is to emphasize the rooted nature of so-called authoritative texts and authors, undermine epistemic finality, widen the ugly ditch of human interpretive dilemmas and sources of meaningfulness, and claim that access to the real is an illusion. From this perspective, the stress is on the importance of communally (or individually) established practices and narratives. Consequently, people recognize the separation between our inherited epistemic solutions (whether in a text, a person, or a magisterium) and the very real levels of cognitive dissonance in their own lives. The thick nature of this response is simply the other side of the philosophical coin.

Both responses are shaped, whether negatively or positively, by the long-standing quest for autonomy from tradition, contingency, and received dogma. The result is the so-called spatial distinction between the private (religious discourse) and the public (secular discourse). The problem of competing religious authorities, traced back to at least the sixteenth and seventeenth centuries, led to a search for a better way of achieving agreement in the public arena. Appeals to accepted opinions of religious authorities eventually played a diminished role in matters of public discourse.

The irony, however, is that the conceptual moves of the past quest for autonomy (and perhaps the current versions) were shaped by antecedent historical traditions (Descartes's indebtedness to the Platonic-Augustinian tradition, for example).[44] The attempt to purify thought of its historical contingency represents a failure to account for antecedent historical traditions. Furthermore, the fact that we still suffer some of the same forms of epistemic anxiety as our intellectual ancestors seems to imply that we have failed to see such proposals in their proper context.

For example, understanding Descartes's project in its context might help us to determine whether his "problem is, in any important sense, *our* problem and, therefore, whether his response still demands the kind of attention it once did." This approach just might free us from our "compulsion to be Cartesian."[45]

To some extent our current epistemic questions and problems are similar to those of our intellectual ancestors, but in other ways our situation is different. One difference, for example, is that we live in a time when appeals to epistemic finality make less and less sense. I am not sure what to call this, but a common impulse is perhaps to rethink the relationship between epistemological approaches and formative practices. This move is complex, scary, and exciting. How does one proceed under the current epistemic dilemma? For some, the price of admission, under the quest for autonomy, entailed losing a thickly conceived locus of authority; for others, the crisis simply confirmed the impression that incommensurable standpoints were inevitable; for still others, the situation warrants a new call for putting forth more adequate accounts of how public space is to be renegotiated.[46]

The point here is not to map out the full details of the crisis. I simply want to note that the effects of the crisis seem to be very much with us, especially as we try to navigate a course that stipulates the conditions for handling the tensile relationship between the thick and the thin. This is at the heart of thinking through what an integrative habit of mind entails in this kind of setting. How, then, ought we to proceed under such a crisis? Do we simply adhere to the intellectual strategies of our own community, fortify the walls, or at least add thicker layers of insulation? Or do we seek to overcome the rubbish of the ages, and thereby try to find some pristine and authentic expression of our humanity? What role does epistemic dependence play? Do we opt for the stance of radical autonomy, refusing to trust any claim until we have the preponderance of evidence independent of appeals to authoritative sources?

The problem of adjudication certainly precipitates the human aspiration for a solution that enables cognitive agents, whether religious or nonreligious, to take on challenges such as relativism, competing claims of authority, and interpretive differences. A desire of this sort is not unique to any one field of knowledge. History, for example, is replete with attempts to crown plausible candidates as the queens and kings of public discourse. Perhaps this is a sign of our unwillingness to acknowledge our finitude, contingency, and tradition-specific ways of being in the world. In saying this, I am not suggesting a Rortian over-dose of irony and contingency, but rather, my analysis essentially agrees with Jeffrey Stout's: the modern flight from authority seeks to find an uncontaminated epistemic space. It is within this context that I offer my constructive proposal.

AN EMBODIED PARTICULARISM OF INFORMED JUDGMENT—A MATTER OF REGULATIVE PRACTICES

A shift in emphasis, as I have intimated, may generate new possibilities for thinking about epistemic reflection and conduct within a pluralistic setting. Changing the focus to regulative practices, however, does not bypass meta-questions about authority and autonomy; it simply targets the question of how people ought to conduct themselves epistemically in a pluralistic setting. Thus, I want to give greater attention to the actual processes, materials, and intellectual virtues that guide epistemic reflection and conduct. As I hope to show, exaggerated claims of autonomy and unhealthy appeals to authority impede this kind of inquiry. Both stances reflect the ongoing influence of the crisis. One stance tries to find a thinly agreed-upon rationale without the baggage of the past, while the other stance seeks to thicken its narrative.

A possible antidote to these extremes may be found in what I am calling an embodied particularism of informed judgment.[47] Cognitive agents, with their particular commitments, engage in an extended conversation with people from radically different perspectives and com-munities. However, informed judgment does not entail an unhealthy appeal to authority, nor does it bracket tradition-specific ways of being in the world. Rather, informed judgment tries to map out an alterna-tive understanding of the relationship between the thick and the thin aspects of epistemic reflection and conduct.[48] Moreover, it links rigorous reflection and intellectual formation. Contemporary work along these lines has shown the extent to which the divorce between philosophical discourse and intellectual formation (and spiritual formation) is a fairly recent development.[49]

Informed judgment draws attention both to the contextual factors that shape epistemic reflection and to the evaluative qualities that en-able people to engage in substantive forms of inquiry while seeking to acquire a connected view. Knowing how to think about, reason through, and understand complex issues presupposes induction into a set of practices, commitments, virtues, skills, and dispositions. In my context, for example, as a graduate professor of theology and philosophy I invite students to participate in a process of philosophical reflection and intellectual formation, rejecting the assumption that the latter is essentially unrelated to the former. In other words, the intellectual virtues fit within the broader framework of forming human agents. I have found that students, whether religious or not, value the emphasis on the intellectual virtues as a fruitful avenue for guiding the intersection of thick and thin commitments. Regardless of perspective, I challenge students to follow virtuous practices such as intellectual honesty, open-mindedness, epistemic humility, intellectual courage, and so on.

Cultivating this kind of inquiry requires a social context in which people who seek knowledge, understanding, and wisdom follow closely and carefully the ongoing conversation about fundamental issues, render apt evaluations of different arguments and interpretations, and form a more comprehensive account of things. Restricting the intellectual virtues to the material content of specific fields of knowledge is not my concern here, especially since methodological procedures, first principles, levels of training, conceptual commitments, and pedagogical goals are certainly bound to differ. The intellectual virtues are no replacement for domain-specific forms of training, but they seem especially "relevant to any discipline, and ought to be of interest to anyone who seriously seeks to transmit knowledge," cultivate the life of the mind, acquire understanding, and pursue wisdom.[50] Thus, agreement on a set of intellectual virtues—interest in truth, intellectual honesty, concern for evidence, capacity to listen to and follow counterarguments, the ability to see how things hang together—opens up the possibility of exchange among people of differing commitments.

A clarification of terminology may help. A regulative approach to epistemology focuses principally on the questions of how intellectual and social practices guide and shape the formation of cognitive agents and of how intellectual virtues contribute to cognitive flourishing. In this regard, Robert Roberts and Jay Wood have recently proposed a regulative approach to epistemology that gives particular attention to individual intellectual virtues. Drawing from Nicholas Wolterstorff's work on Locke, they note the distinction between "rule-oriented" (e.g.,

Descartes's) and "habit oriented" (e.g., Locke's) versions of regulative epistemology. The former concentrates on the "procedural directions for acquiring knowledge, avoiding error, and conducting oneself rationally," while the latter focuses on the "habits of mind of the epistemically rational person" or on the process of "*training* that nurtures *people* in the right intellectual *dispositions*."[51] Notwithstanding the different emphases here, the common ground lies in the attempt to provide an apt "response to perceived deficiencies in people's intellectual conduct" and therefore to "generate guidance for epistemic practice."[52]

The aim of a regulative approach to epistemology, constructively envisioned by Roberts and Wood, is not to employ the virtues to resolve traditional problems in epistemology such as the debate between externalism and internalism, the problem of skepticism, or the dispute between foundationalism and coherentism; nor is it to identify the necessary and sufficient conditions of these character traits. Rather, the goal is to provide an extended analysis of particular virtues (such as love of knowledge, intellectual firmness, courage and caution, humility, autonomy, generosity, and practical wisdom) and, in so doing, to enlarge "our practical understanding of the inner workings of the intellectual life." Seen in this way, a regulative approach to epistemology is "particularly attentive to the character traits of the excellent epistemic agent."[53]

The query, then, is not simply whether a person necessarily needs to be intellectually virtuous to know that *p* and to disseminate *p*. Moreover, my emphasis on the regulative aspect of epistemic reflection and conduct does not intend to squelch the autonomy of the intellectual agent. In fact, concentrating on the question of how the pursuit of intellectual excellence ought to be guided implies protecting people from the ongoing challenge of intellectual vices such as intellectual dishonesty, rash judgments, arbitrary appeals to authority, fudging the evidence, and unwillingness to hear challenging and alternative arguments either in or outside the classroom. A properly formed person is able to decipher when it is necessary to rely on the insights of others, how to respond to criticism, and how to develop one's own thinking, which is never really in isolation. In other words, it is the intellectually virtuous practices that, ideally, make epistemic freedom possible.

The point here is to give due attention to the fact that cognitive agents are both social and autonomous beings. In terms of the social dimension of intellectual formation, it is entirely reasonable to grant fundamental authority to the expertise of others. For example, people new to a field need to learn the ropes, so their deference to those who have acquired informed judgment makes sense and seems entirely reasonable. However, the goal of such a process is to equip people to form their own judgments, not to make them slaves to the insight of others.

Richard Foley perceptively captures the relationship between epistemic dependence (the social process of deferring to people of informed judgment) and autonomy (evaluation of claims, arguments, and so on):

> Despite the influence of others—indeed, because of it—we become intellectually independent, at least if all goes well. Our intellectual training develops and hones abilities that allow us to make autonomous judgments. To be sure, we cannot entirely shake off the influence of others, but no plausible notion of autonomy requires us to do this. What autonomy does require is that we be capable of evaluating, and sometimes even radically criticizing, the views, procedures, and standards of those around us.[54]

A person who acquires mature competence in a particular area is now able "to perform well without the kind of regulation or direction that is needed in early stages of development."[55] Presupposed here is the insistence on judgment—not simply an appeal to rules or principles—as a crucial element of rendering apt assessment of the issue at hand. This is what Newman calls the cultivated form of the illative sense (or complex assent) in the *Grammar*, wisdom in the *University Sermons*, and a connected view in *The Idea of a University*. The appeal here is to "those who by long acquaintance with their subject have a right to judge" (*GA* 269).

A person of informed judgment does not assume that "one size fits all," given that diverse settings—a university, various ecclesial communities, or broader publics of society, for example—call for domain-specific levels of training, different methodological procedures, and wide-ranging modes of public discourse. In addition, informed judgment does not suggest servile deference to authorities as the solution to an epistemic crisis within a pluralistic context. Rather, it demands the capacity to form arguments, map out questions, and pursue greater levels of understanding. Intellectual cloning is foreign to what I have in mind here. Epistemic dependence—gathering insights from others—is certainly fundamental to intellectual formation, and in fact it seems unreasonable to see this phenomenon as detrimental to one's intellectual integrity.

Part of intellectual formation, then, entails showing people that the desire for truth, the love of knowledge, and the search for understanding and wisdom involve determining whether belief-forming processes, practices, and people yield true beliefs over false ones and contribute to the expansion of intellectual horizons. The hope is that people motivated by such a desire will be more likely to conduct thorough inquiries, scrutinize evidence carefully, investigate numerous fields of study, and consider alternative explanations. Another part of intellectual formation requires that cognitive agents identify and learn from sources of informed judgment that are crucial to their cognitive development. Rarely do people form apt judgments about concrete matters in isolation. On the contrary, they take into account feedback from other sources of informed judgment and proceed to see how things hang together in relation to the particular issue or question at hand. As noted earlier, epistemic dependence is not a subtle version of authoritarianism; it simply refers to the maturation process in which epistemic agents, under the tutelage of recognized experts, learn to assess arguments, evaluate evidence, and form their own conclusions.

Such a process includes other intellectual virtues. I mention four. First, people who strive to be intellectually honest tackle difficult questions without seeking simple answers; they acknowledge the limits of their knowledge and their understanding while tenaciously trying to expand both. However, people who ignore complex and difficult questions only solidify intellectual vices such as intellectual dishonesty, close-mindedness, and rash judgments. These vices preclude the possibility of refining our thinking and of participating in conversations with others. Second, people who desire to be open-minded take seriously different ideas and counterarguments, recognizing that being impulsive in assessing evidence fosters intellectual deficiencies and hinders intellectual growth, both personally and communally. They realize that amassing and presenting knowledge includes persistence, discipline, patience, and wisdom. Third, intellectual courage requires, among other things, the willingness to defend one's position while also considering other perspectives. Tenacity certainly plays a role in sustaining one's position, but it should not be confused with close-mindedness. Last, people who pursue understanding seek to grasp how insights from various fields of knowledge hang together, and they decipher how to incorporate these insights into their current base of knowledge. Thus, understanding entails the capacity to connect various pieces of data, practices, and experiences into a synthetic judgment.

Obviously, the goals of informed judgment are multifaceted. One goal may be the acquisition of true beliefs. In this regard, the desire for truth may involve virtues such as intellectual honesty, epistemic humility, tenacity, and courage, but the primary aim here is to decipher whether a belief is true. Understanding, as another goal of informed judgment, certainly includes pursuing truth and thereby presupposes knowledge (a person knows that p) as an important component. However, a person can know many pieces of information and not necessarily grasp how they fit together in light of one another.[56] Furthermore, a more important goal of understanding is to see how various pieces of data hang together in light of one another. The result is the expansion of one's epistemic horizons, and not simply an accumulation of isolated pieces of information. Both knowledge and understanding are crucial to the pursuit of informed judgment. They are especially important for equipping people as much as possible to acquire truth and to see beyond their own perspective, thereby making the crucial connections among diverse ideas and resources.

We have met countless people who know that p but fall short in the areas of understanding and wisdom. We have also met people who have profoundly internalized the virtues of humility, courage, and intellectual honesty but fail to acquire knowledge that p. Ideally, we hope that the subjective and the objective come together in the epistemic agent. But this goal does not imply that intellectual virtues are necessary and sufficient for acquiring knowledge. With an integrative habit of mind as our end, intellectual formation is integral to guiding how people ought to engage in epistemic conduct.

Informed judgment, then, envisions the task of cultivating cognitive agents that can move from particular commitments to broader forms of discourse both within a community and among radically different communities. The capacity to connect the thick and the thin is at the heart of an embodied particularism of informed judgment. It pushes people to link new and existing knowledge to the relevant questions, issues, and subject matters at hand. Consequently, it makes sense to expect people to operate from particular starting points, but it does not follow that their beliefs, commitments, practices, and judgments should be protected from being interrogated. In fact, people who are interested in pursuing truth, knowledge, understanding, and wisdom ought to extend their particular claims to the varied public spaces of human discourse.

An embodied particularism of informed judgment, therefore, zooms in on the social and intellectual conditions under which people actualize an integrative habit of mind—the capacity to see how things fit together in light of one another and how an understanding of this sort relates to the situation at hand. However, my use of the term "social" does not suggest the overextended view that desiderata such as knowledge, truth, rationality, justification, understanding, and wisdom are simply a social construct or simply what our peers will let us get away with. On the contrary, my proposal focuses on the requisite evaluative capacities of cognitive agents within a particular context. In this regard, the social dimension challenges the "Cartesian image" in which people inquire, evaluate arguments, and pursue knowledge as isolated and autonomous individuals. Such an image "ignores the interpersonal and institutional contexts in which most knowledge endeavors are actually undertaken."[57]

As a result, informed judgment challenges notions such as authoritarianism and epistemic individualism. It seems reasonable, at least prima facie, for people to trust select individuals and associated communities that have shaped their current way of thinking and being in the world, but it also makes sense to operate with some level of suspicion about these thick commitments. However, it does not follow that either option alone fully captures the ongoing task. On the one hand, a radical conception of autonomy (a person acquires knowledge independently) fails to explain both how our intellectual training actually occurs and the extent to which others have contributed to a person's knowledge and understanding of things. On the other hand, a radical appeal to tradition-specific forms of belief-formation is equally problematic. Such a posture rarely enables people to get out of the house, view the broader landscape, and explore critically both internal and external claims. We start from somewhere in terms of our training, our knowledge of various subject matters, our different methodological commitments, and our awareness of interpretive issues. Nevertheless, an important goal is to help people learn to think, write, and argue in ways that show healthy respect for other sources of knowledge while making informed judgments of their own. What I am after here is an integrative habit of mind (instantiated as an embodied particularism of informed judgment) that is deeply particularistic and genuinely committed to a more expansive form of human discourse.

The cultivation of informed judgment demands a host of critical interlocutors and therefore presupposes the capacity to extend personal judgments to communal spheres of discourse. For example, if pursuing truth is a personal matter, what prevents ideological distortions and intellectual vices from setting in or becoming entrenched in one's own thinking? However, these same tendencies can be systemic in communities. In fact, an appeal to the communal over against the personal or to the personal over the communal is not an immediate remedy for intellectual vices. We have seen intellectual abuses on both personal and communal levels.

Instead, informed judgment calls for the intersection of the communal and the personal undergirded by a persistent commitment to intellectual integrity. For instance, intellectual freedom is a valued good, but it does not imply exemption from engaging others in honest and open discussion, nor does it mean that acknowledging dependence upon other sources of informed judgment necessarily shrinks the space of one's intellectual freedom. Both individual and communal dimensions need regulative processes. The virtues function as regulative pointers about how both individuals and communities ought to conduct the process of intellectual inquiry. The importance of communal learning is the capacity to extend the self into a more expansive way of seeing, knowing, and understanding things, and the importance of autonomy is for individuals to learn to incorporate insights from others without such a process turning into something like groupthink or authoritarian dictates from on high.

My suggestion here is not really new; it is steeped in a long-standing tradition, both in its Christian and non-Christian versions (Aristotelian, Stoic, Christian, and so on), and I think it has some constructive ties with Newman's basic proposal about human cognition and intellectual formation. It also calls us to revisit the rich contours of religious and philosophical traditions and explore ways in which these resources may serve as resources of healing. Pursuing a proposal of this sort may be a painful experience, especially given the ongoing manifestations of the epistemic crisis, but it may result in profound forms of transformation in the various publics of reflection.

We must resist the temptation to equate any one methodology, epistemology, or approach with the content and identity of the Christian faith, however. The narrowing of perspective that accompanies such an equation partly explains the resistance to religion and, I think, eventually results in commensurate forms of scientism, secularism, and fundamentalism. Canonizing an epistemological theory is not the answer; it simply exacerbates the crisis. Rather, reconnecting our intellectual practices with the healing practices of religion seems more promising. This does not imply backing away from rigorous thinking; rather, it simply locates our intellectual projects within a set of vibrant materials, persons, and practices.[58]

With my proposal of an integrative habit of mind (materialized as an embodied particularism of informed judgment) I seek to unpack the conditions under which formative practices, people, and habits transform the self and thereby identify a process for cultivating human excellence. More specifically, an integrative habit of mind is not simply about following rules or fulfilling one's epistemic duty but entails the ability to make salient connections. It is deeply needed, given current manifestations of the ongoing crisis of authority. Such a move requires the power to discern what matters and what is relevant for our context. It calls for people to decipher a proper fit between the subject matter and the particular kind of audience they encounter.

Digesting isolated pieces of information is no replacement for the synthetic component of discernment, understanding, and wisdom. The capacity to connect various insights and experiences into a coherent understanding of how they fit together is an acquired skill. With this in mind, one challenge ahead is to come to grips with the crisis, find the appropriate resources of healing, and foster human agents of informed judgment.

The capacity to see how things fit together in light of one another and how an understanding of this sort relates to the situation at hand is at the center of an embodied particularism of informed judgment. One can decipher how things fit together in light of one another without explicit awareness of how such pattern recognition actually happens. Contemporary parallels can be found in reliabilism and recent work in cognitive science.[59] The pursuit of wisdom, shaped by the goal of forming an integrative habit of mind, also demonstrates the importance of mature probing into faith, honing the uncultivated illative sense into an informed level of judgment. In other words, Newman's account of human cognition does not hibernate in the world of the tacit and implicit. He focuses on the different levels of cognition, which helps give different nuances to the discussion. It is now time to work out the reflective and unreflective components of an integrative habit of mind.

Chapter Two

A MATTER OF PROPER FIT

"For the educated person seeks exactness in each area to the extent that the nature of the subject allows; for apparently it is just as mistaken to demand demonstrations from a rhetorician as to accept [merely] persuasive arguments from a mathematician."
—Aristotle, *Nicomachean Ethics*

"Wisdom cannot mean constant reflection. A wise person must be guided by her reflective values in some sense, but being a reflective agent does not mean engaging in deep contemplation and justification of one's projects at all times."
—Valerie Tiberius, *The Reflective Life*

Another feature of an integrative habit of mind involves understanding how different aspects of cognitive activity (such as tacit and cultivated forms of judgment) relate to the particular situation at hand. In this regard, the distinction between uncultivated (unreflective) and cultivated (reflective) dimensions of the illative sense in the *Grammar of Assent* connects, to some extent, with the current epistemological discussion about internalism and externalism. The illative sense, for Newman, is principally a natural faculty of judgment, and it has both unreflective and reflective levels. The unreflective kind of cognitive activity combines phenomena without awareness of how things obtain; the reflective kind, as a result of training and the cultivation of complex assent, deciphers how various pieces of data fit together in light of one another. Working through this distinction has significant implications for the constructive task of pursuing wisdom.

However, my aim in this chapter is not to resolve the contemporary epistemological debate between internalism and externalism, nor do I argue that Newman necessarily had the exact terminology in mind. Rather, what I glean constructively from the distinction between the uncultivated and cultivated forms of the illative sense is a matter of proper fit. It is true that the larger project of the *Grammar* is to show that assent without full understanding and without demonstrative proof of *p* is rationally acceptable, which thus highlights to some extent the externalist feature of reliable belief- and judgment-forming processes. However, the tacit and implicit dimensions of belief- and judgment-formation clearly belong on the larger canvas of human cognition, and so to categorize these processes amounts to seeing them as different modalities of cognitive activity (that is, implicit and explicit ways of reasoning and rendering judgments, informal and formal kinds of inference). An internalist component lingers beneath the surface in the *Grammar*. When the intellectual chips fall, Newman argues for a higher level of reflection in his conception of cultivated judgment (that is, what he describes as complex assent in the *Grammar*, as a connected view or the enlargement of mind in *The Idea of a University*, and as wisdom in the *University Sermons*). Consequently, in this chapter I will focus largely on the cultivated form of the illative sense in the *Grammar* while probing its connection with the contemporary discussion.

In the first section, I clarify the extent to which Newman's distinction between the uncultivated and cultivated forms of the illative sense relates to the externalist and internalist debate.[1] However, I shift the focus here to what a distinction of this sort means for developing an account of cultivated judgment (not necessarily what it means for fleshing out an account of justification or knowledge per se). In the second section, I suggest that Newman's philosophy of cognition warrants a constructive link with recent work in cognitive science and epistemology. In the third section, I argue that cultivated judgment is deeply connected to the intellectual character of the cognitive agent. The cultivated level of the illative sense involves deliberative and finely honed activities with the aim of securing a more comprehensive understanding of things. In the fourth section, I show how an appeal to proper fit undergirds my attempt to connect, at least constructively, Newman's conception of cultivated judgment and the contemporary discussion about reflective and unreflective facets of human cognition. In essence, proper fit—as an instantiation of an integrative habit of mind—highlights the context- and agent-specific aspects of human cognition and, in our case at hand, of cultivated judgment.

FRAMING THE ISSUE

The activity of the uncultivated illative sense generally fits the externalist emphasis on reliable belief- and judgment-forming processes. It is largely equivalent to the process of acquiring rationally acceptable beliefs or making apt judgments, though the cognitive agent is not internally aware of the relevant factors, states, and conditions that justify those beliefs and aptly form those judgments.[2] In this sense, these processes of belief- and judgment-formation may be "more or less implicit, and without direct and full advertence of the mind exercising it" (*GA* 233). One may be justified in holding a belief or in rendering a judgment, though whatever makes it justified (or an apt judgment) is external to one's cognitive grasp.[3]

However, these automatic belief- and judgment-forming processes—the state of being justified in holding a belief or making tacit judgments about the issues at hand, for example—are subject to further reflection and refinement (the activity of providing reasons for believing that *p* or rendering cultivated judgments about *p*), especially when the aim is to decipher how these beliefs and judgments fit together in light of one another.[4] This is precisely where the cultivated illative sense enters the discussion. It generally fits an internalist emphasis on epistemic evaluation in the sense that some factors, motivational states, and conditions are accessible to the person on this level. The cognizer, from a first-person point of view, reflectively investigates whether the grounds of particular beliefs are valid, whether they can be overthrown by sufficient reasons, and whether they fit within a larger circle of knowledge and understanding.[5] This kind of cognitive activity stems from maturation of the illative sense, which comes through experience, practice, and guidance from exemplars of cultivated judgment.

Accordingly, an integrative habit of mind includes objective (factors or processes external to a person's perspective) and subjective (factors or processes of which a person is aware) conditions under which people form beliefs and render apt judgments.[6] With this sort of distinction in mind, Newman describes the illative sense as "a natural, uncultivated faculty," an "acquired habit" (*GA* 261, 278), "good sense," "common sense," an "implicit" process of reasoning "without the direct and full advertence of the mind exercising it" (*GA* 233), "a higher logic" (*GA* 240), "supra-logical judgment," "*judicium prudentis viri* [the judgment of prudent people]" (*GA* 251), "the architectonic faculty," "right judgment in ratiocination" (*GA* 269), a "special faculty" to be perfected (*GA* 281), "the reasoning faculty, as exercised by the gifted, or by educated or otherwise well-prepared minds" (*GA* 283), the "sole and final judgment on the validity of an inference in concrete matter" (*GA* 271, 276), and the power of determining the convergence of "probabilities" (*GA* 282).[7] Overall, the illative sense combines various pieces of data into a synthetic understanding and forms an apt judgment about the relevant issues at hand. Its cultivated form enables the cognitive agent to recognize when to rely on externalist processes and when to engage in rigorous internalist evaluation.

Missing the distinction between unreflective and reflective activities of the illative sense has contributed to depictions of Newman as a skeptic, as a fideist, as a subjectivist, and as a relativist.[8] This oversight, to put it in contemporary terms, fails to assess the externalist and internalist features of the illative sense as different epistemic desiderata. For example, acquiring a judgment in a truth-conducive manner (without grasping the factors that aptly form that judgment), and explaining how various judgments fit together in light of one another, are both desirable for developing a fuller account of cultivated judgment.[9] I hope to show that a closer reading of Newman's conception of cultivated judgment, especially as it is fleshed out in the *Grammar*, challenges such impressions. The issue at hand is not whether it is better to cultivate informed judgments but whether the absence of reflective awareness precludes such a judgment from being aptly formed.

Unpacking the distinction between unreflective and reflective dimensions of the illative sense clarifies the context- and agent-specific aspects of rendering apt judgments about the issues at hand. Both of these aspects of the illative sense have a proper place in the intellectual formation of the self, though they have distinctive features or aims. In other words, not all facets or features of belief- and judgment-formation should be placed exclusively into one of these categories (either reflective or unreflective), nor should we reduce every situation to the activity of one dimension or feature of the illative sense. Thus, knowing how each modality of human cognition functions in particular situations, as the occasion arises, requires a cultivated judgment of proper fit.[10] An evaluation of this sort requires the wisdom to assess correctly what is required for the situation at hand.[11]

NEWMAN'S PHILOSOPHY OF COGNITION— A CONTEMPORARY LINK

Human cognition, for Newman, functions at least on two levels. On a basic level, people form beliefs reliably and make apt judgments without appealing to explicitly stated grounds or, to put it in contemporary terms, without fulfilling some "prior grounding requirement."[12] They recognize "facts without assignable media of perceiving," and as a result, "propositions pass before [them] and receive [their] assent without [their] consciousness [reflective endorsement]" (GA 263, 157).[13] Accordingly, a person believes that p without employing the full-blown powers of justification (without providing reasons for believing that p), or at least, not all processes of belief- and judgment-formation are subject to that person's epistemic perspective.

Newman's account of tacit and implicit kinds of human cognition bears a certain resemblance to what cognitive science calls automaticity.[14] On this unreflective level, people render judgments, process various pieces of data, and make efficient decisions without cognitive awareness of how such processes obtain. As Timothy Wilson points out, a picture emerges of "a set of pervasive, adaptive, sophisticated mental processes that occur largely out of view."[15] Although mental processes of this kind "are immediately inaccessible to consciousness," they still "influence judgments, feelings, and behavior." In fact, this modality of human cognition is "capable of learning complex information, and indeed, under some circumstances it learns information better and faster than our conscious minds."[16] The uncultivated form of the illative sense is similar to this kind of cognitive activity. On this point, Newman says that it "is difficult to avoid calling such clear presentiments by the name of instinct." Such terminology is acceptable if we mean by it the capacity to perceive things without "recognizable intellectual media of realization" (Ward 2:258).

As Wilson puts it, once we recognize that "people can think in quite so-phisticated ways nonconsciously, however, questions arise about the relation between conscious and nonconscious processing." How does one divide the labor "between these two parts of the mind?"[17] Although Newman's context is certainly different from the contemporary world of cognitive science, he anticipates the same kind of inquiry about the unreflective and reflective aspects of human cognition and about the task of thinking through the division of cognitive labor.[18] Both Newman's account of the tacit and im-plicit aspects of the illative sense and the contemporary cognitive scientific depiction of automaticity seem to call into question full-blown voluntarist accounts of belief- and judgment-formation. This kind of cognitive activity connects situations without the human agent necessarily having explicit awareness of how such pattern recognition actually happens.

However, appealing to automatic or unreflective aspects of belief- and judgment- formation is not the end of the story. Newman's philosophy of cognition includes a reflective character, which involves explaining how these beliefs and judgments fit together (or cohere) in light of one an-other. In so doing, Newman distinguishes this kind of cognitive activity from passive and automatic belief- and judgment-forming processes.[19] Understanding how things fit together in light of one another requires the exercise of mature thinking, which is refined by practice, experience, and disciplined reflection. It is rationally acceptable for cognitive agents to presume that their belief- and judgment-forming processes and fac-ulties are trustworthy unless they have reason to think otherwise.[20] As the notion of complex assent (cultivated judgment) will show, however, the epistemic features of right judgment in reasoning and of seeing how things fit together in light of one another from an internalist angle (first-person point of view) occur when the context demands it.

Newman's twofold conception of human cognition, therefore, seems relevant to the contemporary conversation. As we have seen, human cognition entails two distinct modalities. The first modality (implicit reasoning) refers to the process by which people form beliefs or judg-ments without explicit awareness of their grounds. The second modality (explicit reasoning, cultivated judgment) refers to the activity of specify-ing the grounds of beliefs and judgments and of spelling out how they fit together in light of one another. As we shall see, the cultivation of the illative sense as a mature and deliberative form of reasoning engages in the task of articulating reasons for our beliefs and judgments.[21]

Newman's account also couples normative inquiry with phenomeno-logical analysis of belief- and judgment-formation. In essence, he argues that the normative should be informed by—but not confused with—the phenomenological. Accordingly, conceptions of human cognition must both (1) take into account the actual conditions under which people reason and form judgments within real-world environments and (2) target the question of how they ought to engage in epistemic reflec-tion. Missing the distinction between the uncultivated and cultivated dimensions of the illative sense explains the collapse of an important but subtle difference between the descriptive and the normative. As noted, the uncultivated dimension presupposes the reliability of belief- and judgment-forming processes, and the cultivated dimension calls for the maturation of cognitive capacities and evaluative qualities such as right judgment in reasoning, explaining how things fit together in light of one another, intellectual honesty, open-mindedness, and willingness to engage in rigorous investigation and evaluation.

A person motivated by the goal of forming an integrative habit of mind recognizes the different aspects of human cognition and certainly knows how to think through the level of expertise sufficient for addressing the particular issue at hand. Pursuing knowledge, truth, justification, un-derstanding, and wisdom, at least on a higher level of cognitive activity, has a regulative link to what intellectual exemplars do. Cultivated judg-ment combines reliable processes and virtuous dispositions, relocating relevant normative properties of beliefs to more fundamental evaluative qualities of cognitive agents. Such activities are certainly concerned with the logical status of beliefs, but the intellectual character of the inquirer plays an equally important part in seeing how things fit together.

In saying this, I do not intend to solve all of the interpretive issues associated with Newman's philosophy of cognition and his philosophy of mind. I simply point out that he notes different aspects of cognitive activity and correlates different modalities of reasoning with particular issues at hand. In this sense, the pursuit of wisdom, grounded in and shaped by the desire to cultivate an integrated habit of mind, distin-guishes between unreflective and reflective aspects of human cognition and gives each its proper due.[22] Each facet of human cognition seems to be context- and task-specific. Everyday beliefs and judgments are usually formed through unconscious pattern recognition, though they certainly are subject to evaluation. In fact, appeal to tacit and implicit kinds of cognitive activity will inevitably raise questions about how we know that these processes do, in fact, form true rather than false beliefs and how we understand the way in which the relevant pieces of data fit together in light of one another. This is where cultivated judgment enters the discussion.

CULTIVATED JUDGMENT

Cultivated judgment is fundamentally connected to the intellectual character of the cognitive agent. The aim here is not simply to acquire true beliefs and to avoid false ones, though this is certainly an important pursuit. Rather, the cultivated level of the illative sense involves deliberative and finely honed activities with the aim of securing a more comprehensive understanding of things. In a letter to Henry James Coleridge, Newman states that the link between a proper state of mind and intellectual principles is fundamental to how he envisions epistemic reflection and conduct: "My book [The *Grammar*] is to show that a right moral state of mind germinates or even generates good intellectual principles" (*L&D* 25:280).[23] However, the former (a right moral state of mind) does not necessarily produce the latter (good intellectual principles). If this is what Newman means, counterexamples certainly can be produced.

Newman highlights, in *The Idea of a University*, how a properly formed and trained intellect acquires a "connected view or grasp of things" (*Idea* XLIII). Experience, practice, praiseworthy dispositions, and disciplined reflection are fundamental to guiding this kind of epistemic reflection and conduct. For example, the cognitive activities of determining whether our inferences yield truth or error in concrete matters and of seeking to understand how things fit together in light of one another presuppose "the trustworthiness of the illative sense" (*GA* 281). The focus here is on how environmental conditions and evaluative qualities (such as the intellectual character of the cognitive agent [*GA* 240]) shape the process of rendering a cultivated judgment about concrete matters. The personal dimension of the illative sense does not disappear in the processes of belief- and judgment-formation; it is simply developed into a more refined form of judgment.

What Newman seems to be getting at is similar to Robert Brandom's observation that "the capacity for such reasoning is not to be identified exclusively with mastery of a logical calculus."[24] On the one hand, cognitive processes responsible for generating "assent, action, and certitude, are in fact too multiform, subtle, omnigenous, too implicit, to allow of being measured by rule" (*GA* 240). On the other hand (at least on the reflective level of human cognition), properties of beliefs are not divorced from the evaluative qualities of the cognitive agent.[25] A robust conception of an integrative habit of mind plays an important role in guiding the process of intellectual exchange. More precisely, the path to wisdom calls for the enlargement of mind and the formation of a connected view.

Although the illative sense functions sometimes as "a natural uncultivated faculty," an integrative habit of mind calls for the cultivation of this faculty of judgment (*GA* 261). The cultivated dimension of the illative sense is "an acquired habit, though it has its origin in nature itself, and is formed and matured by practice and experience" (*GA* 278). In other words, an integrative habit of mind requires "perfection" of the illative sense or maturation of "right judgment in ratiocination" (*GA* 269, 271). Belief-forming faculties such as memory, perception, and reason are necessary for this kind of judgment, but they need to be used and trained in such a way as to enable the cognitive agent to apply relevant insights to the particular issue at hand.[26]

The cultivated illative sense, to some extent, bears a resemblance to "Aristotle's φρόνησις," though the former's target is the "inquisitio veri."[27] Newman, like Aristotle, recognizes the domain-specific nature of cultivated judgment. Cognitive agents must embody "a special preparation of mind" to acquire skillful judgment in each "department of inquiry and discussion" (*GA* 321). However, the activity of the illative sense is not confined to moral decision-making (τὰ πρακτά).[28] It "holds good in all concrete matters, not only in those cases of practice and of duty, in which we are familiar with it, but in all questions of truth and falsehood generally" (*GA* 251). Such an observation implies a long-term process by which cognitive agents form apt judgments about matters in a particular field of knowledge.

However, humans do not perpetually pay close attention to the processes of belief- and judgment-formation. Constant awareness and epistemic regulation seem impossible, impractical, and unreasonable. As Christopher Hookway points out, our explicit modes of reflection do not govern all the workings of cognition, nor do they monitor, prima facie, all facets of belief- and judgment-formation:

Our participation in activities generally depends upon mastery of a practice: education provides us with a body of habits, routines, dispositions, which enable us to engage in activities without reflecting upon what to do at each turn. Indeed, the knowledge of how to proceed that is implicit in our habitual practices often far outreaches what can be made explicit through reflection. . . . Perhaps, as philosophers, we can make this implicit knowledge explicit . . . but our normal inability to do this is no loss; indeed it probably contributes to our success. Confidence in our practical capacities does not require us to be able to articulate what is going on and understand how they work. We exercise our judgement in thinking about what to do without being able to identify the principles on which we depend, and this is not a cognitive failing. These platitudes about how we carry out practical activities generally can cast illumination on the internalism/externalism debate.[29]

Though in a context far removed from Hookway's, Newman makes a similar move. First principles, for example, are a part of our cognitive lives, and from an externalist point of view we are justified in proceeding this way until we are convinced otherwise.

We also assess the status of our beliefs and judgments, deciphering if we have sufficient reasons for holding them. In this regard we formulate a set of intellectual virtues for regulating epistemic conduct, and our regulative practices presuppose the capacity to engage in such activity. In the *Grammar*, Newman refers to rigorous evaluation of our assumptions, practices, beliefs, inquiries, and intellectual qualities as complex assent (cultivated judgment). The internalist component of complex assent surfaces in Newman's claim that certitude "is the perception of a truth with the perception that it is a truth, or the consciousness of knowing, as is expressed in the phrase, 'I know that I know'" (*GA* 163). In my estimation, scholars have overlooked this element of Newman's thought in the *Grammar*. Perhaps some of his arguments for the indefectibility of assent, which at times seem to conflate an ontology of truth with epistemology, explain such an oversight. Nevertheless, the distinction between simple (unreflective) and complex (reflective) assents seems to hold promise, especially in terms of the contemporary discussion of how to negotiate externalist and internalist features within real-world environments.

What Newman targets here, as he does in *The Idea of a University*, are the social, intellectual, and environmental conditions under which cognitive agents see how things fit together in light of one another and how the resultant synthetic judgment relates to the issue at hand. Desire alone is insufficient for determining whether a person's beliefs have a greater probability of being true rather than false, for discerning how things fit together in light of one another, and for instantiating an integrative habit of mind. A person's beliefs and synthetic judgments must comport with the objective features of the world (*GA* 293) and not simply reflect a subjective state of mind. "By an assent to a proposition as true, I mean the assertion of my intellect, that what it is contemplating subjectively, has an existence outside me."[30] Overall, Newman's account of uncultivated and cultivated judgment acknowledges the distinction between truth and epistemic processes: "If by certitude about a thing is to be understood the knowledge of the truth, let it be considered that what is once true is always true, and cannot fail, whereas what is once known need not always be known, and is capable of failing. It follows, that if I am certain of a thing, I believe it will remain what I now hold it to be, even though my mind should have the bad fortune to let it drop" (*GA* 163). It seems that Newman grants that truth is incorrigible, but our attempts both to secure the grounds of a belief and to track the basic belief-forming processes are fallible.[31]

Ernest Sosa makes a similar distinction between animal knowledge and reflective knowledge. Such a distinction may be a helpful way of thinking through how Newman differentiates between the uncultivated and cultivated forms of the illative sense. On the one hand, animal knowledge is aptly formed belief, though with little or no reflection on the part of the cognizer. This kind of knowledge does not require that one have an epistemic perspective from which to determine the justification-making properties of a belief. On the other hand, reflective knowledge demands not only that a belief be aptly formed but also that it must fit "coherently within the epistemic perspective of the believer."[32]

Sosa's description of reflective knowledge strikes me as something comparable to what Newman calls wisdom in the *University Sermons*, a connected view in *The Idea of a University*, and the cultivated illative sense in the *Grammar*. Though animal knowledge "can be obtained through the use of truth-conducive mechanisms," reflective knowledge requires coherentist justification—the capacity to see how things hang together.[33] Sosa does, in fact, claim that one has reflective knowledge when "one's judgment or belief manifests not only such a direct response to the fact known but also understanding of its place in a wider whole that includes one's beliefs and knowledge of it and how these come about."[34] Thus, some of the epistemic values that differentiate reflective knowledge from animal knowledge include understanding, coherence (explanation), and the capacity to arrive at "the truth through our own intelligent doings, by relying on our own reliable abilities, skills, and faculties."[35]

The point here is not to say that Sosa's distinction between animal knowledge and reflective knowledge fully captures Newman's distinction between uncultivated and cultivated aspects of the illative sense. As John Greco points out, however, Sosa's notion of reflective knowledge is more like understanding (perhaps what I am calling the reflective or cultivated aspect of an integrative habit of mind) than knowledge per se.[36] The link with Sosa is in terms of Newman's distinction between uncultivated and cultivated forms of the illative sense. In this sense, Sosa's distinction seems somewhat comparable.

The standard interpretation is to see Newman's argument in the *Grammar* as a defense of rationally acceptable belief without full understanding and without demonstrative proof of *p*. John Lamont, for example, rightly points out that Newman's basic moves in the *Grammar* are intended to correct these internalist presuppositions.[37] Such an observation certainly gets at a fundamental concern in the *Grammar*. Nevertheless, the conception of complex assent is an important aspect of what Newman characteristically calls wisdom in the *University Sermons* (e.g., Sermon XIV) and a connected view in *The Idea of a University*. Cultivating the illative sense presupposes the importance of exemplars— perhaps cognitive agents of wisdom—for discerning salient facts, experiences, and arguments (*GA* 248, 278). In this respect, Newman follows Aristotle's observation that skillful judgment comes from giving "heed to the undemonstrated sayings and opinions of the experienced, not less than to demonstrations, from their having the eye of experience, they behold the principles of things" (*GA* 268). In other words, a person of cultivated judgment "has developed an eye for deciphering what is salient in concrete situations."[38]

As we have seen, Newman acknowledges that on a basic level the illative sense enables people to form beliefs reliably or to render apt judgments without awareness of how these beliefs are justified and how these judgments are aptly formed. Informal inference, for example, is "a process of reasoning [that] is more or less implicit, and without the direct and full advertence of the mind exercising it" (*GA* 233). Such reasoning is a "clear and rapid act of intellect, always, however, by an unwritten summing-up" (*GA* 232). This mode of reasoning does not supplant "the [formal] logical form of inference, but is rather one and the same with it; only it is no longer an abstraction" (*GA* 232). Thus, some conclusions are not reached by "any possible verbal enumeration of all the considerations, minute but abundant, delicate but effective, which unite to bring him to it; but by a mental comprehension of the whole case, and a discernment of its upshot" (*GA* 232).

Belief- and judgment-forming processes, however, do not stop here. At times, explaining how one's beliefs and judgments fit together in light of one another (that is, an integrative habit of mind in the pursuit of understanding and wisdom) involves something more than a simple appeal to basic belief- and judgment-forming processes. A properly disposed mind coupled with the requisite intellectual habits creates greater possibilities for moving from a particular to a more comprehensive understanding of things. Forming a complex assent of this sort stems from a responsible outgrowth of educational and social commitments. Proper training through regulative practices enables the mind to perfect its ratiocinative powers. Hence, Newman sees a difference between a proper and an improper use of the illative sense. Cultivation of the illative sense, in other words, "is not furnished by how most people use their ratiocinative powers. It is determined by how those who have *perfected* them do so."[39]

So, belief- and judgment-forming processes are not exempt from error; in the process of reasoning and rendering judgments we discover and discard errors. Faulty reasoning, for example, does not justify radical doubts about these belief- and judgment-forming processes. The same logic also applies to the reliability of belief-forming faculties such as memory, introspection, and sense perception.[40] Although these faculties fail us occasionally, we still depend on them as sources for acquiring truth, knowledge, understanding, and wisdom. Presupposed here is a set of intellectual practices that develop these basic belief-forming processes and that correct misuses.

What seems to be the case for Newman is that a person may acquire rationally acceptable beliefs or may render apt judgments unreflectively. Such a commitment inevitably leads to a form of articulation, especially if the occasion warrants that the epistemic agent ought to explain how such a belief or judgment contributes to and fits within a more comprehensive way of understanding things.[41] In this regard, complex assent differs from simple assent in that it seeks to uncover cognitive infelicities and to determine explicitly whether our beliefs and judgments form a connected view. Such processes of investigation require the exercise of cultivated judgment ("mature judgment"). In fact, Newman argues that "in the case of educated minds, investigations into the argumentative proof of the things to which they have given their assent, is an obligation, or rather a necessity" (*GA* 160). [42] The combination of "practice and experience" enables humans to fulfill their epistemic obligation toward cognitive excellence (*GA* 189). [43] The proper function of the intellect—"a growth in the use of those faculties by which knowledge is acquired"— warrants disciplined reflection, experience, practice, and the insights of epistemic exemplars (*GA* 189).

As a natural faculty of judgment, the illative sense determines how various pieces of data converge into a synthetic understanding of the issue at hand. It regulates the process of human inquiry, deliberation, and argument about concrete matters, combining the motivational states (desire for truth, understanding, and wisdom) and basic belief-forming processes (memory, sense perception, and reason). Yet the illative sense has a personal dimension and is materialized through training, history, and the intellectual demeanor of the inquirer. [44] Such a focus does not eliminate questions concerning knowledge, justification, and truth. It simply maintains that a finely honed focus on cognitive agency creates a greater understanding of the process of inquiry, deliberation, and evaluation. This particularistic move necessitates greater work in philosophical and theological anthropology.

Although he acknowledges that interpretive differences emerge from the intellectual character of cognitive agents gathered around the table, Newman rejects subjectivism, relativism, and fideism as real options. Intellectually virtuous people disagree precisely because of the context- and agent-specific aspects of their intellectual formation. So the formation of an integrative habit of mind, especially in terms of the distinction between uncultivated and cultivated aspects of the illative sense, does not necessarily guarantee agreement among people from radically different perspectives and commitments. Moreover, the reality of interpretive differences does not imply the nonexistence of "objective truth" (*GA* 293). As we have seen, complex assent involves determining whether an assent is "objectively true as well as subjectively" (*GA* 162). To overstate Newman's focus on belief formation without demonstra-tive proof and without full understanding misses the cultivated dimension of the illative sense. Complex assent presupposes a deliberate and explicit attempt to render right judgment in reasoning about concrete matters. The subjective and objective dimensions of the cognitive agent merge in complex assent.

At the end of the day, Newman's conception of complex assent (cultivated judgment) challenges accounts of judgment that ignore the role played by reflection in evaluating beliefs, inquiries, and intellectual qualities. Newman also rejects accounts that equate rationally acceptable beliefs or judgments only with full access to what makes them true, justified, or aptly formed. His conception of complex assent grants that internal motivation of epistemic reflection (the desire to fulfill one's epistemic duty) and basic belief-forming processes both play a role in the epistemic enterprise. The search for truth, knowledge, understanding, and wisdom—as envisioned in the distinction between simple and complex assents—presumes the formation of a cognitive agent.

There are many flavors of externalism and internalism. My point in this chapter, then, is not to find an exact match between the versions of externalism and internalism and Newman's basic distinction between uncultivated and cultivated forms of the illative sense. Instead, the more relevant emphasis is that not all situations warrant a first-person perspective (an internalist kind of epistemic reflection). Uncritically received, the internalist demands seem out of touch, and this is precisely what Newman in the *Grammar* identified as a mistake.

Newman seems to offer a complex portrait here, challenging the options of (1) epistemic egoism (one is justified in believing or rendering judgments about *p* if and only if one arrives at this independently of other sources) and (2) a full-blown deontological conception of evidentialism (one is obligated to ensure that one's beliefs are justified or one's judgments are aptly formed).[45] In this regard, Newman deals with the question of epistemic obligation according to the level and demeanor of the cognitive agent. One is obligated to explore how one knows that *p* if and only if one has the capacity, resources, and time. Such an observation certainly includes internalist and contextualist insights. In other words, Newman takes the situation as fundamental to tackling the question of epistemic obligation, although he realizes that faculties and processes not always present to one's noetic awareness play a fundamental role in the formation of beliefs and that they are generally, though not infallibly, reliable in giving epistemic agents accurate information about the world.

CULTIVATED JUDGMENT AS A MATTER OF PROPER FIT

An appeal to proper fit undergirds my attempt to connect, at least constructively, Newman's conception of cultivated judgment and the contemporary discussion about reflective and unreflective aspects of human cognition. In essence, the notion of proper fit highlights the context- and agent-specific contours of human cognition and informed judgment. It presumes what Stephen Hetherington describes as the diversity of abilities and skills:

> Abilities can take different *forms*. (i) Some are manifested in a partly or wholly 'automatic' way. For instance, when a batter is well able to play a particular sort of shot, his exercising this ability could require him not to think, or even to be able to think, about playing the shot when doing so. The shot must be performed, not only in apt circumstances, but *wholly unreflectively*. Any accompanying reflection—even the person's still being able to reflect at that moment—would interfere with his playing the shot well, no matter how otherwise apt the circumstances happen to be. Now imagine an ability, having that kind of structure, being directed at registering that *p*. This would make any such registering justified in an *externalist* way. For example, there would be an actual *reliability*—and without any accompanying reflection on that reliability—in the person's ability to register accurately that *p*. (ii) Some abilities, in order to be exercised effectively, *do* involve either the actuality or the availability of mental monitoring—checking, evaluating, reasoning, and so forth. An ability like this, when directed at accurately registering that *p*, will make any such registering justified in an *internalist way*. For example, good evidence would be used reflectively in generating and in evaluating whether to maintain, the registering.[46]

The first form (automatic and unreflective cognitive activities) parallels largely the activity of the uncultivated illative sense. Yet monitoring how one assesses evidence is fundamental to the pursuit of truth, knowledge, understanding, and wisdom; such activity (complex assent, for example) needs to be regulated through a set of intellectual practices and parallels the second form. In other words, reasoning-giving practices are fundamental to making sense of one's beliefs, showing how they form a coherent way of thinking and being in the world, and how such a synthetic account relates to the issue at hand. Undergirding the diversity of skills is a communal division of labor.[47]

Paul Moser offers a comparable distinction between these cognitive activities and couches the current debate between externalism and internalism (about rationality, reasons, and obligations) in terms of constructive instrumentalism:

> One's aims, or purposes, in adopting and using a notion of rationality, reasons, or obligations can cogently recommend, at least to oneself, an internalist or externalist notion of rationality, reasons, or obligations. If, on the one hand, we now aim to evaluate attitudes and actions from one's actual evidential and motivational standpoint, we do well to use an internalist notion of rationality, reasons, or obligations. If, on the other hand, we now aim to evaluate attitudes and actions from a position independent of one's actual motivational standpoint, we need to use an externalist notion of rationality, reasons, or obligations. A single person, moreover, might use an externalist notion for certain purposes and an internalist notion for other purposes.[48]

Cultivated judgment, in similar fashion, can be constructively imagined as a nuanced version that employs externalist and internalist features when the situation demands the appropriate option. It recognizes that there are different aims and goals (perhaps what contemporary epistemologists call desiderata). In this sense, internalist and externalist features may be viewed as complementary (and not necessarily oppositional), at least in terms of developing an account of cultivated judgment.

Heather Battaly offers a comparable observation about the terrain of virtue epistemology. She argues that the distinction between "virtue reliabilism" (intellectual virtues are stable natural faculties such as sense-perception, memory, induction, and deduction) and "virtue responsibilism" (virtues are acquired traits such as open-mindedness, intellectual courage, and humility) parallels the difference between low and high grades of knowledge. In terms of this distinction, virtue reliabilism is better suited for explaining low-grade knowledge (e.g., perceptual knowledge that is acquired passively) while virtue responsibilism is better suited for explaining high-grade knowledge (e.g., an epistemic agent needs the character traits of open-mindedness, intellectual courage, and conscientiousness for engaging in epistemic evaluation). In reference to low-grade knowledge, intentional activity on the part of the epistemic agent is not required. In this regard, adults "share low-grade knowledge with children and, perhaps, other animals. In contrast, high-grade knowledge is acquired actively, rather than passively, as a result of intentional inquiry."[49]

Cultivated judgment, understood in terms of proper fit, likewise sees the need both for identifying practices and processes that are truth-conducive (perhaps analogous to what epistemologists describe as reliabilism) and for deciphering how things hang together (perhaps analogous to what epistemologists describe as explanation or understanding). In terms of focusing on the conditions under which people form apt judgments, an integrative habit of mind includes both factors or processes external to a person's perspective and factors, states, or processes of which a person is internally aware. Not all factors, states, and processes that aptly form judgments need to be internally accessible to the cognitive agent, yet the formation of an integrative habit of mind includes an internalist element. For instance, Newman's notion of complex assent presupposes a connection between praiseworthy dispositions (such as the desire to fulfill one's epistemic duty, intellectual honesty, and epistemic humility) and the goal of discerning coherence-making relationships (such as seeing or explaining how various pieces of information fit together in light of one another). The complexity of concrete situations warrants a division of labor in which some engage in reflective assessment of the epistemic issues at hand and others participate in reliably formed practices and processes. This kind of epistemic dependence is empirically grounded in everyday life.

My constructive link between Newman's conception of cultivated judgment and recent work on the unreflective and reflective aspects of belief- and judgment-formation may help navigate some of the current landscape of scholarship. Instead of dividing cultivated judgment into purely subjective and objective dimensions, we may learn to see how these dimensions fit concrete situations. Also, Newman's project in conversation with recent epistemology does not get tangled in the internalist and externalist web. Rather, lingering in the *Grammar* is an implicit move to sort out the internal and external components of the cognitive agent in complex assent, especially when warranted by the situation.[50] Consequently, an account of cultivated judgment resists both a radical subjectivist posture that ignores the objective conditions of beliefs and an extreme objectivist position that eclipses the subjective conditions of intellectual formation. The cognitive agent interested in knowledge, truth, understanding, and wisdom must be open to assessing his or her own claims.

Newman's notion of cultivated judgment requires a fuller account of the processes under which human agents engage in deliberate epistemic reflection. Along these lines, his idea of cultivated judgment seems to fit recent questions about the role of wisdom and understanding in the enterprise of epistemology.[51] As Newman intimates, cultivated judgment involves a vibrant set of practices, habits, and exemplars of informed judgment. For example, recognizing salient facts and offering a synthetic judgment of various pieces of data are not strictly rule-governed. Rather, each "involves an aspect of knowing-how that is partially learned by imitation and practice."[52] Cultivated judgment enables cognitive agents to detect how things fit together; isolated bits of information alone will not nurture the synthetic imagination.

The goals of ascertaining true beliefs and avoiding false ones, then, are not the only and the highest goods that define a person of cultivated judgment. For example, the fundamental difference "between merely believing a bunch of true statements within subject matter M, and having understanding of M (or some part of M), is that one somehow sees the way things 'fit together.'" Human agents of cultivated judgment are not merely "collectors of random or trivial truths."[53] As Newman points out, there are people "who contemplate things both in the mass and individually, but not correlatively, who accumulate facts without forming judgments, who are satisfied with deep learning or extensive information" (US 288).

The distinction between uncultivated and cultivated forms of the illative sense has an Alexandrian flavor to it. Newman was profoundly shaped by the principles of reserve and economy articulated by Clement of Alexandria and Origen. These principles correlate epistemic pursuits with the actual capacity of the individual. They seem to be governing Newman's distinction between the cultivated and uncultivated forms of the illative sense. He saw the importance of perceiving the gradations of understanding and of different modalities of reasoning. The task of the human agent of wisdom, in this regard, is "to be acutely sensitive to the needs of the person who will receive the knowledge."[54] It seems that the contemporary application comes in terms of knowing when we need to explain how we know what we know while also acknowledging the importance of following reliable belief-forming processes.

Consequently, an integrative habit of mind, shaped by the notion of proper fit, recognizes that the noetic makeup of the human person includes unreflective and reflective cognitive activities. A person formed in this way understands that sometimes the situation warrants conscious deliberation and sometimes it does not.[55] On the one hand, the tendency to understand the reflective aspect as the only basis for wise decision making ignores the fact that not all aspects of human cognition are subject—nor should they be—to this kind of evaluation. Much of our daily decision making is grounded in the unreflective exercise of recognition abilities, following both established social cues and reliable belief-forming faculties such as memory, perception, and testimony.[56] Few are afforded the time and knowledge requisite for considering a vast range of data and rendering adequate assessment of complex problems.

On the other hand, the reflective aspect is crucial to being epistemically responsible and expanding horizons. To emphasize only the unreflective aspect of human cognition is to ignore the fact that the process of forming apt judgments about concrete matters is fallible and can be corrected by explicit reasoning. Those who see the value of pursuing cultivated judgment are obligated to show how their beliefs hang together in light of one another, especially when they are engaged in dialogue with interlocutors. The desire for a comprehensive view of things requires that cognitive agents be open to challenges, and if challenges occur, they must be able to meet them and make the requisite revisions. People of cultivated judgment, in other words, recognize that their beliefs "can be made articulate and (we hope) improved."[57]

In terms of human cognition, an important feature of an integrative habit of mind begins with the conditions under which cognitive agents pursue knowledge, truth, understanding, and wisdom. Cognitive activities of this sort call for a robust account of intellectual formation. The highest good includes much more than the achievement of true beliefs and the avoidance of false beliefs; it requires understanding important truths, deciphering how they cohere within real-world environments, and seeing how they transform the self. An integrative habit of mind understands this distinction and relocates the search for truth, knowledge, understanding, and wisdom, moving the search from a list of abstract notions to a concrete quest for the ground of all things. Hence, an integrative habit of mind does not stop at the world of justified true beliefs but seeks to understand how things hang together in light of one another and in relation to the question at hand. This comment is not a rejection of the epistemic projects of defining and mapping out the phenomena of knowledge, justification, and truth but rather expands the focus of epistemology to include the value of the knower and the role of understanding.[58]

A person shaped by the goal of forming an integrative habit of mind recognizes the distinction between the implicit and explicit modes of belief- and judgment-formation. The implicit mode certainly does not necessitate the explicit grasp of the reasons for which a person forms beliefs and judgments. The problem here is that some disqualify Newman because he fails to meet the criteria of an internalist epistemology, or they overstate his externalist moves. However, Newman's account of cultivated judgment, constructively envisioned, is a matter of proper fit.

—— *Chapter Three* ——

A CONNECTED VIEW

"Every person who is actually absorbed in any given form of experience is by the very absorption committed to the opinion that no other form is valid, that his form is the only one adequate to the comprehension of reality. Hence arise discords; for when artists and scientists, who after all do inhabit a common world of fact, meet and discuss their aims, each is apt to accuse the other of wasting his life on a world of illusions."
    —Robin G. Collingwood, *Speculum Mentis or The Map of Knowledge*

"Whatever else the task of education, it should not drive the intellect and the imagination of students into channels that seem to become narrower as our century grows older; consequently, it should do everything possible to make it easier for those engaged in one discipline to understand the methods, achievements, hopes, ambitions, frustrations, the intellectual and emotional processes, of those working in other fields."
    —Isaiah Berlin, *The Power of Ideas*

In unearthing and developing themes from select texts in the corpus of Newman's writings, I have argued thus far that the pursuit of wisdom, grounded in and shaped by the goal of cultivating an integrative habit of mind, gives greater attention to the conditions under which human cognition actually works and to the role that evaluative qualities play in regulating epistemic reflection and conduct. As a fundamental motivation and activity, an integrative habit of mind does not stipulate that cognitive agents ought to thin out or bracket their thick commitments before engaging in conversation about the issues at hand. At the same time, to highlight the thick character of epistemic reflection and conduct does not mean insulating one's claims from other perspectives. In fact, broadening one's horizons is indispensable to the processes of acquiring greater levels of understanding and of learning to make apt judgments about the relevant issues.[1] An emphasis of this sort also involves seeing the unreflective and reflective aspects of human cognition as a matter of proper fit. Consequently, providing a more adequate understanding of the tensile relationship between the thick and the thin is crucial to the pursuit of wisdom.

In this chapter I hone the focus a bit and argue that an additional feature of an integrative habit of mind involves forming a connected view. More specifically, I argue that forming, sustaining, and embodying a connected view is fundamental to the pursuit of wisdom within a university context. In this regard, I link Newman's notion of a connected view in *The Idea of a University* and the ongoing task of formulating an adequate philosophy of education for our time. In particular, I offer some suggestions concerning the kind of teachers and researchers that my proposal of a connected view envisions within a university setting. I include my own experiences and thick commitments as a graduate professor of theology and philosophy while drawing insights from different publics (e.g., university and society) and fields of knowledge (e.g., history, philosophy of education, cognitive science, ethics, religion, and epistemology).

The scope of my proposal includes teaching and research, even though I do not address in detail the question of how these activities intersect with one another in the context of a university.[2] Rather, I argue that those entrusted with teaching and research responsibilities ought to pay greater attention not simply to state-of-the-art techniques and learning outcomes but, rather, to the intellectual formation of persons.[3] Such an emphasis requires that we revisit our understanding of (1) the aims and scope of intellectual formation in a university environment, (2) our existing teaching and research practices, and (3) our presuppositions about what it means to realize and carry out an integrative habit of mind within our current educational setting.

As a result, in this chapter I first argue that a central task of the educational process, in Newmanian terms, entails acquiring a connected view.

The correlative possibility between Newman's context and our own lies in his insistence on the importance of forming in learners a connected view and on the significance of pedagogical exemplars for shaping educational practices within a university context, not necessarily in his fuller vision of what a university ought to be.[4] Second, I clarify what it means to realize and carry out a connected view within an educational setting. The milieu of the university must be saturated with people that exemplify a connected view. Third, I argue that pedagogical wisdom entails the capacity to draw salient connections and to show how they relate to the context of the learning environment at hand. Envisioned here is an embodied pedagogy that seeks to form and sustain a vibrant community of inquirers.

Fourth, I show how interdisciplinarity, as intimated in the notion of a connected view, fosters the pursuit of wisdom in our educational context today. The aim here is (1) to cultivate an environment of face-to-face interaction with people from different perspectives and disciplines, (2) to engage in a set of intellectual habits and practices such as inter-departmental colloquia, and (3) to promote an ongoing pursuit of mutual understanding and wisdom in team-taught classes and in collaborative research projects.[5] Transmitting information is not enough to achieve these goals. Interdisciplinarity of this sort is both timely and difficult, and this is precisely the reason why pedagogical and research exemplars are indispensable to our contemporary educational setting.[6]

ACQUIRING A CONNECTED VIEW

Acquiring "a connected view or grasp of things" (*Idea* XLIII) in a university setting entails a process of intellectual training and formation in which people enlarge their educational horizons through disciplined and systematic reflection. As a result, they become apt at (1) grasping the "mutual positions," "bearings," and "true relations" of various pieces of information in light of one another (*Idea* 34, 101); (2) discerning what others have failed to perceive and understand;[7] and (3) showing what this kind of understanding means for the situation at hand. An integrative capacity of this sort is "an acquired faculty of judgment, of clear-sightedness, of sagacity, of wisdom, of philosophical reach of mind, and of intellectual self-possession and repose" (*Idea* 115). As Newman points out, people are not equipped to comprehend the vast expanse of knowledge at "a single glance, or gain possession of it at once" (*Idea* 34). Rather, the evaluative process in which cognitive agents make connections occurs by "piecemeal and accumulation . . . by the comparison, the combination, the mutual correction, the continual adaptation, of many partial notions, by the employment, concentration, and joint action of many faculties and exercises of the mind" (*Idea* 114).

Newman's brief account of wisdom in the *University Sermons* furnishes the basic framework for his notion of a connected view in *The Idea of a University*.[8] In particular, Sermon XIV, "Wisdom, as Contrasted with Faith and Bigotry," maps out the difference between narrow-mindedness and the pursuit of wisdom. For Newman, narrow-mindedness constricts thought, hinders the formation of a connected view, and as a result, impedes the pursuit of wisdom:

> Narrow minds have no power of throwing themselves into the mind of others. They have stiffened in one position, as limbs of the body subjected to confinement, or as our organs of speech, which after a while cannot learn new tones and inflections. They have already parcelled out to their own satisfaction the whole world of knowledge; they have drawn their lines, and formed their classes, and given to each opinion, argument, principle, and party, its own locality; they profess to know where to find every thing; and they cannot learn any other disposition. They are vexed at new principles of arrangement, and grow giddy amid cross divisions; and, even if they make the effort, cannot master them. They think that any one truth excludes another which is distinct from it, and that every opinion is contrary to their own opinions which is not included in them. . . . None are so easily deceived by others as they who are preoccupied with their own notions. They are soon persuaded that another agrees with them, if he disagrees with their opponents. They resolve his ideas into their own, and, whatever words he may use to clear his meaning, even the most distinct and forcible, these fail to convey to them any new view, or to open to them his mind. (*US* 307–309ff.)

Conversely, wisdom (the conceptual equivalent of a connected view in *The Idea of a University*) entails an "orderly and mature development of thought" (the process of forming and evaluating beliefs), a "comprehensive view of things" (an integrative grasp of how various pieces of data fit together in light of one another), and an "enlargement or expansion of mind," that is, broadening horizons (*US* 279, 282; see also *Idea* 94).

Cultivating an intellectual posture of this sort fosters a safeguard against intellectual vices such as dogmatism, fanaticism, narrow-mindedness, making rash judgments, arbitrary appeals to authority, fudging the evidence, and unwillingness to hear challenging and alternative arguments in and outside of the classroom, especially since these vices hinder the processes of broadening horizons and of cultivating a connected view.

Rethinking the aims and scope of the educational process in this way calls into question the kind of reductionism that seeks to comprehend fully various issues through a single glance, whether such a mind-set manifests itself in the forms of religion, science, literature, morality, aesthetics, politics, psychology, philosophy, history, sociology, education, anthropology, archaeology, and so forth. John Kekes offers a similar observation concerning the philosophical impulse (or absolutist mind-set) that undergirds a reductionistic kind of thinking in the context of determining essentially what the good life entails:

> The philosophical problems that concern us here have their origin in some disruption of everyday life that seriously interferes with our attempts to live good lives. Science, history, religion, aesthetics, morality, and subjectivity are particular attempts to cope with these disruptions. But these attempts often conflict with one another because they propose incompatible ways of coping. The absolutist approach to resolving these conflicts is to formulate a general outlook derived from one of these attempts and then assign it precedence over other general outlooks. A mode of reflection then is a general outlook that aims to understand the true significance of the relevant facts. This approach will not resolve these conflicts, however, because the defenders of each mode of reflection claim that precedence should be assigned to the mode that is based on the particular attempt at coping with the disruption that they favor.[9]

There is a real temptation to see everything exclusively through one's domain-specific lenses or to think that one's preferred mode of reflection is superior to all others on almost every issue. This kind of thinking, for example, shows up in the decision-making process about developing a core curriculum, about funding research projects, and about determining what best accomplishes the vision of a university. Such a mind-set, however, actually impedes students, faculty, and administrators from acquiring a more comprehensive understanding of things and thereby forming a connected view. This is precisely the reason it is crucial to show how a regulative epistemology guides teaching and research practices for the task of cultivating the kind of people that embody an integrative habit of mind within a university setting.

Narrowness of perspective in due course takes a deep hold on those who try to make their "particular craft usurp and occupy the universe" (*Idea* 44). Teachers, researchers, and students shaped in this way deem their own mode of reflection as the "centre of all truth, and view every part or the chief parts of knowledge as if developed from it, and to be tested and determined by its principles" (*Idea* 63). Such people feel compelled to say something about "every subject; habit, fashion, the public require it of them: and, if so, they can give sentence according to their knowledge" (*Idea* 57). Contracted pursuits of this sort, however, actually get in the way of gaining greater levels of understanding of the subject at hand. They turn out to be nothing more than obstacles to perceiving and assessing things beyond domain-specific commitments.

Thomas Nagel describes a similar way of thinking, expressed in current versions of reductionism, in a chapter on "Evolutionary Naturalism and the Fear of Religion." He opens the chapter by stating that he finds congenial Charles Sanders Peirce's depiction of rational inquiry, undergirded by a kind of realism and antireductionism (truths do not depend on our minds but on nature). However, adopting this philosophical position makes it difficult to avoid wondering whether the metaphysical picture associated with rationalism will be "religious, or quasi-religious. Rationalism has always had a more religious flavour than empiricism." In fact, the realization that the "relation between mind and world is something fundamental makes many people in this day and age nervous." Such anxiety, according to Nagel, is "one manifestation of a fear of religion which has large and often pernicious consequences for modern intellectual life."[10]

Nagel then spells out the consequences of this kind of fear of religion, which can be so deeply laden in a person that he or she may not only reject belief in God but also hope and desire that there is no God:

> In speaking of the fear of religion, I don't mean to refer to the entirely reasonable hostility toward certain established religions and religious institutions, in virtue of their objectionable moral doctrines, social policies, and political influence. Nor am I referring to the association of many religious beliefs with superstition and the acceptance of evident empirical falsehoods. I am

talking about something deeper—namely, the fear of religion itself. I speak from experience, being strongly subject to this fear myself: I *want* atheism to be true and am made *uneasy* by the fact that some of the most intelligent and well-informed people I know are religious believers. It isn't just that I don't believe in God, and, naturally, *hope* that I'm right in my belief. It's that I *hope* there is no God! I don't *want* there to be a God; I don't *want* the universe to be like that [my emphasis].

One can sense the psychological tone of Nagel's observation; the language of want, desire, uneasiness, and hope stems from an irrational fear, the result of which is the attempt to reduce everything to a conceptual glance, to a field of knowledge, or to a methodology. As he points out, a cosmic crisis of authority of this kind (such as a person who does not want there to be a God) is not an uncommon condition. In fact, it may be "responsible for much of the scientism and reductionism of our own time."[11]

While Nagel rejects a reductionistic version of naturalism, especially when driven by the aforementioned fear, he does not resort to theism as his alternative.[12] He finds "the religious proposal *less* explanatory than the hypothesis of some systematic aspect of the natural order that would make the appearance of minds in harmony with the universe something to be expected." Nevertheless, he offers a similar kind of penetrating analysis of reductionism as Newman did within his own context. One contemporary manifestation of reductionism, Nagel adds, can be seen in the "ludicrous overuse of evolutionary biology to explain everything about life, including everything about the human mind."[13] Undergirding this kind of reductionism is "an epistemological criterion of reality—that only what can be understood in a certain way exists." Nagel's antidote to reductionism is to "resist the intellectual effects of such fear (if not fear itself), for it is just as irrational to be influenced in one's beliefs by the hope that God does not exist as by the hope that God does exist."[14]

A Newmanian commitment to the process of enlarging intellectual horizons and thereby developing a connected view shares some of the same observations, concerns, and criticisms, though from a religious point of view. Without safeguards, reductionism can easily operate out of fear and pretend to capture complex issues through one disciplinary glance. In contrast, a person with an expansive intellect develops an eye for deciphering salient connections, "referring [many things] severally to their true place in the universal system, understanding their respective values, and determining their mutual dependence" (*Idea* 103). An intellectual posture of this kind compares, systematizes, and weaves ideas from domain-specific areas of inquiry and seeks to render a coherent understanding of the issue at hand. Although coming from different methodological assumptions and ways of proceeding, people in domain-specific fields of inquiry, motivated by the goal of acquiring a connected view, share common ground in pursuing truth, knowledge, understanding, and wisdom.

An emphasis on forming and sustaining a connected view also challenges the notion that utility alone drives the aims and goals of education. Proficiency in drawing insights from different fields of knowledge and in seeing how they hang together may be pursued for its own sake, not simply for professional advancement. "When the intellect has once been properly trained and formed to have a connected view or grasp of things, it will display its powers with more or less effect according to its particular quality and capacity in the individual" (*Idea* XLIII).[13] Accordingly, the university inducts students into a set of regulative practices with the aim of training them to reason proficiently in different disciplines, participate in truth-conducive practices, acquire greater levels of understanding, make interdisciplinary connections, and embody a holistic way of being in the world. Undergirding all of these activities is the praiseworthy desire to become a paragon of "intellectual excellence" (*Idea* 92, 95).

Newman developed a notion of the enlargement of mind and provided the rationale for acquiring a connected view of the relevant issues in domain-specific areas of inquiry:

> The enlargement [of mind] consists, not merely in the passive reception into the mind of a number of ideas hitherto unknown to it, but in the mind's energetic and simultaneous action upon and towards and among those new ideas, which are rushing in upon it. It is the action of a formative power, reducing to order and meaning the matter of our acquirements; it is a making of objects of our knowledge subjectively our own, or, to use a familiar word, it is a digestion of what we receive, into the substance of our previous state of thought; and without this no enlargement is said to follow. There is no enlargement, unless there be a comparison of ideas one with another, as they come before the mind, and a systematizing of them. . . . It is not the

mere addition to our knowledge that is the illumination; but the locomotion, the movement onwards, of that mental centre, to which both what we know, and what we are learning, the accumulating mass of our acquirements, gravitates. . . . I have accordingly laid down first, that all branches of knowledge are, at least implicitly, the subject-matter of its teaching; that these branches are not isolated and independent one of another, but form together a whole or system: they run into each other, and complete each other, and that, in proportion to our view of them as a whole, is the exactness and trustworthiness of the knowledge which they separately convey. (*Idea* 101, 162–163)

Newman argues at great length that the mind needs to be carefully trained in order to make connections across the disciplines and to pursue truth-conducive practices. As we have seen, narrowly focused ways of proceeding fail both to connect domain-specific insights with other fields of knowledge and to recognize their own limitations. In contrast, a philosophically mature mind strives to understand particular rules of procedure in different fields of knowledge and the internal logic of domain-specific areas of inquiry, but it is elastic enough to seek and implement complementary insights from other fields of knowledge.

Another way of putting this is to see how domain-specific insights fit within the larger circles of knowledge, understanding, and wisdom. Interdisciplinary thinking (as we will see) plays a crucial role in broadening intellectual horizons. Hence, the charge to students and faculty is to participate together in relevant practices of the university, that is, conduct thorough inquiries, scrutinize evidence carefully, investigate numerous fields of study, and consider alternative explanations. The "desideratum" of the university starts with "the force, the steadiness, the comprehensiveness and the versatility of intellect, the command over our own powers, the instinctive just estimate of things as they pass before us, which sometimes indeed is a natural gift, but commonly is not gained without much effort and the exercise of years" (*Idea* XLII). How a person maps out and addresses critical issues within a university setting is tied to the internalization of the requisite intellectual virtues. So, a robust process of intellectual formation is fundamental to epistemic reflection within this context.

As we have seen, collecting bits of information is not sufficient for expanding horizons, forming a connected view, and making apt judgments about the relevant issues at hand. For example, a great memory does not necessarily produce deeper levels of understanding, nor does the memorizing of grammatical rules necessarily result in proficient translation skills. Moreover, being well read, or well versed in a particular area, does not necessarily rule out the adoption of a narrow perspective. In fact, some people may "hear a thousand lectures," "read a thousand volumes," and yet understand things very much as they did at the beginning of their inquiry (*Idea* 368). In this sense they "embrace in their minds a vast multitude of ideas, but with little sensitivity about their real relations towards each other" (*Idea* 102). People of this frame of mind are satisfied with acquiring and regurgitating large amounts of information. However, they fail to decipher and understand "the respective relations which exist between their acquisitions," and thereby they fall short of forming a connected view of the relevant issues at hand (*US* 289; see also *Idea* 34).

A connected view, therefore, presupposes a trained intellect. The process of forming a connected view in teachers and researchers does not refer simply to the activity of properly functioning faculties such as memory, sense perception, reason, though they are certainly important ingredients. More to the point, a connected view requires an active engagement of the mind, in which people learn through disciplined and systematic reflection to make salient connections. They actively pursue and cultivate proper intellectual dispositions and habits in order to see how things fit together in light of one another, rather than passively receiving "scraps and details" (*Idea* 111):

> However, a very little consideration will make it plain also, that knowledge itself, though a condition of the mind's enlargement, yet, whatever be its range, is not that very thing which enlarges it. Rather the foregoing instances show that this enlargement consists in the comparison of the subjects of knowledge one with another. We feel ourselves to be ranging freely, when we not only learn something, but when we also refer it to what we knew before. It is not the mere addition to our knowledge which is the enlargement, but the change of place, the movement onwards, of that moral centre, to which what we know and what we have been acquiring, the whole mass of our knowledge, as it were, gravitates. And therefore a philosophical cast of thought, or a comprehensive mind, or wisdom in conduct or policy, implies a connected view of the old with the new, an insight into the bearing and

influence of each part upon every other; without which there is no whole, and could be no centre. It is the knowledge, not only of things, but of their mutual relations. It is organized, and therefore living knowledge. (*US* 287)

With a comparative and comprehensive eye, teachers and researchers integrate new insights into existing knowledge, understanding, and wisdom. A connected view is not, therefore, simply an accumulation of isolated facts or adding bits of information to the current stock of ideas. Instead, it requires the capacity to see how components relate to one another and how such an understanding forms a coherent way of thinking and being in the world.[16] Accumulating information from different fields of knowledge, without exploring their relations, does not expand the mind but simply loads it with isolated facts. Such a process of belief formation amounts to "undigested reading" (*US* 289). Without the capacity to integrate, people lack the perspective from which to render informed judgments about concrete matters.

Conceptually, I link the idea of a connected view (constructively gleaned from *The Idea of a University* and the *University Sermons*) with the pursuit of understanding and wisdom, and not merely with knowledge, per se. Joshua Hochschild rightly argues that Newman here is "articulating what Aristotle simply called 'wisdom' or sophia, the highest of the virtues of speculative intellect."[17] So, my constructive modification does not seem to be a stretch but, rather, entails a clarification of terms with some recent insights of epistemology in mind. In this sense, a connected view seems to be an expansion of what Newman describes as the pursuit of wisdom in the *University Sermons*. To put it in contemporary terms, a connected view involves seeing how "coherence-making relationships" form "a large and comprehensive body of information. One can know many pieces of information, but understanding is achieved only when informational items are pieced together by the subject in question."[18] In other words, a connected view involves grasping how individual pieces of data fit together in light of one another. It seems to be conceptually equivalent to the pursuit of understanding and wisdom.

Consequently, an important feature of an integrative habit of a mind involves developing a connected view. To be more precise, teachers and researchers who cultivate a connected view within themselves become adept at (1) grasping how various pieces of data fit together in light of one another, (2) discerning what others have failed to perceive and understand, and (3) rendering a skillful application of these insights to a particular context. The process of acquiring a connected view reflects a move from the particular to the more comprehensive. By exploring the multifaceted terrain of the university through the praiseworthy desire to form an integrative habit of mind, teachers and researchers generate new opportunities to broaden their horizons.

EMBODYING A CONNECTED VIEW

The concept of a connected view just outlined points to a wonderful ideal, but it must be embodied in teachers and researchers. In other words, the milieu of a university must be saturated with people who exemplify a connected view. While *The Idea of a University* unpacks the logic, aim, and shape of university education, the *Rise and Progress of Universities* explains how pedagogical exemplars are indispensable for advancing the aforementioned idea of a university. As Mary Katherine Tillman points out, *Rise and Progress* is a "work of *historical imagination*," especially in its "vivid portraits of particular persons, great institutions, and of flourishing cities and whole cultures."[19] Spelling out what an environment of this sort entails is what Newman had in mind in his vision of the university. The challenge of deciphering the relevant epistemic, social, and environmental conditions that play a role in the process of acquiring a connected view is equally relevant today.

Professorial influence in this regard plays an enormous role in materializing and advancing the formal aims of the university. This educational setting is not merely about conveying facts, or filling people with isolated bits of information or endowing them with professional skills. Rather, the university is a place where teachers and researchers make every effort (1) to form a community of inquirers, (2) to embody a connected view, and (3) to explore the local and global aspects of being educated citizens in this world. A vision of education shaped in this way puts a human touch on the process of intellectual formation within a university environment.

Cultivating a connected view, as we have seen, necessitates a complex network of social and intellectual practices. The picture here is of students entering a diverse world of ideas, consulting living sources of informed judgment, and grasping how things hang together in light of one another. Induction into this kind of environment involves seeing how interaction among teaching and research exemplars—from different commitments, perspectives, and disciplines—produces greater levels of understanding. It is through collaborative efforts that teachers and researchers consider and deal with different points of view and hopefully, as a result, broaden their horizons. They come "to learn different ways of reading a situation and different questions to pose in order to see the picture with increased insight and clarity."[20] Recent work in virtue epistemology, for example, shows how collaborative projects that include people from the fields of ethics, cognitive science, and epistemology can enrich our understanding of traditional issues in epistemology (such as theories of knowledge, justification, externalism, and internalism) and can expand our understanding of the scope and aims of epistemology (such as the role of the intellectual virtues in regulating epistemic conduct, the nature and ground of epistemic goodness, and the contours of the intellectual life).[21]

Forming and embodying a connected view in the life of the university seems increasingly relevant to our own context today. Books alone are incapable of responding to detailed and particular questions on a range of topics and of addressing "the very difficulties which are severally felt by each reader in succession" (*Rise* 9). Edward Craig makes a similar observation. Although mere sources of information "may often be extremely useful, [they] are never actively helpful. How could they be? They don't know what the inquirer is up to."[22] Understanding and wisdom "inhere primarily in people, rather than in the storage facilities of books and computers."[23] Teaching and research, as embodied activities, ought to capture and motivate students to enlarge the social and intellectual dimensions of their personhood and to engage in a passionate and rigorous investigation of a particular subject matter.

A university without teaching and research exemplars, in Newmanian terms, is like an "arctic winter" and the end result is the creation of an "an ice-bound, petrified, cast-iron University, and nothing else" (*Rise* 74). Conversely, a robust vision of the education process presumes that ideas come to life more in "personal documents" than in "dead abstracts and tables" (*Rise* 198). Teachers and researchers vitalize and humanize the subject matter, and as a result, members of the community of inquirers learn how "to engage, delight, and absorb a human intelligence" (*Rise* 186). To put it in more contemporary terms, professors "must know what their acts exemplify, what qualities of life and character they themselves embody, as they try to convey knowledge" and understanding to others.[24] Perceptive integration of the new with the old requires teaching and research exemplars and, if fortunate, perhaps a wonderful combination of both skills in one person. David Ford, for example, points out that "research skills can best be learnt through apprenticeship to those who are at the forefront of their field—if they are willing, and enabled, to teach them."[25]

There is, however, a potential weakness in an emphasis on the influence of teaching and research exemplars, which may foster vices such as intellectual pride, misguided ambition, self-indulgence, and obsession with praise. Along with professorial influence, the university needs to implement collegial accountability. Newman's own recognition of the tension between domain-specific ways of thinking and the pursuit of a connected view is not very far from our own disciplinary turf wars. Forming a connected view is a complex, difficult task in view of the roadblocks mounted by disciplinary claims of superiority. Nevertheless, the ongoing challenge is to create a community of inquirers in which faculty and students recognize discipline-specific issues and challenges while striving to embody a connected view.

THE ART OF LEARNING WITHIN
A COMMUNITY OF INQUIRERS

Pedagogical wisdom—the capacity to draw salient connections and show how they relate to the issue at hand—entails activities distinct from simply gathering various pieces of information. Discernment of this sort, for example, requires knowledge of the assigned readings and the capacity to show how this material relates to the particular issues and questions raised by the class. Unloading pre-established material is no replacement for aptly and skillfully relating knowledge and understanding to particular situations. The desire to cover everything in class usually results in information overload, indicating that the professor is still struggling to discern how to apply knowledge to a particular situation or to adjust course materials to the needs, situations, and issues of the community of inquirers.

Pedagogical and research exemplars of wisdom, then, recognize the difference between imparting information and linking ideas and context in relevant ways. Teachers and researchers invite students to inhabit a shared world of learning and to function as a community of inquirers. Within such an environment, the inquirers seek to become more skilled at assessing sympathetically and critically different theories, interpretations, and arguments—desiring also to learn how to solidify various pieces of data, practices, and experiences into an informed judgment of the issue at hand and how to apply this sort of understanding to particular situations.

It is crucial to spell out what this sort of educational process entails. In my own context, for example, I begin the semester with a commentary on the nature and expectations of the class, along with a discussion of the evaluative qualities requisite for this sort of learning environment. The students and I agree in principle to work together as a community of inquirers, and I have found that patience, tenacity, honesty, and willingness to modify things go a long way with students. To the best of our ability we promise to uphold evaluative qualities such as open-mindedness in appraising data, reflective consideration of other arguments, interest in truth, proficiency in oral and written communication, willingness to learn, epistemic humility, and intellectual honesty. Understood in this way, the art of learning entails a dialogical process by which students and teacher engage one another and the subject matter in terms of self-discovery and expansive thinking.

In terms reminiscent of but slightly different from the Newmanian notion of a connected view, Michael Buckley envisions the process of learning as an attempt to acquire a philosophical grammar. An effort of this sort involves helping a community of inquirers navigate intellectual inquiry and discern a thematic unity among different disciplines. The aim, in other words, is to discover and trace the "common themes that form the presuppositions of" different fields of knowledge, rather than to impose a "systematic unity among them."[26] Buckley captures two basic components of teaching: (1) the ability to connect themes, methodological concerns, and issues across the disciplines, and (2) the capacity to relate the subject matter to the concerns, commitments, and assumptions of students. Such a pedagogical strategy, with its emphasis on thinking through themes from different angles, enables students to have a better sense of what the process of moving from a particular set of assumptions to a more comprehensive understanding of the topic actually entails.

A learning environment of this sort provides concrete ways of following the internal logic of the particular area of study while understanding how to weave isolated facts into a coherent way of thinking. Students observe how the professor melds various pieces of data into a synthetic account of the issue at hand. In this sense, the art of learning entails grasping "patterns of meaningful connection," not simply gathering "isolated data bits."[27] By absorbing the internal logic of a subject matter, students learn to form a connected view, which enables them "to react in appropriate ways to various stimuli and situations."[28]

Unfortunately, students sometimes are led to believe that the aim of education is simply to excavate and regurgitate information from a data bank such as the professor or a text. Conversely, a community of inquirers engages in open and critical evaluation of existing forms of knowledge, understanding, and wisdom. Professors and students committed to this ideal seek to "observe and reflect and speak and listen, with passion and with discipline, in the circle gathered around a given subject."[29] As a result, the classroom becomes an environment in which the professor, along with students, participates in a vigorous and informed conversation about the subject matter. Nevertheless, a problem emerges, for example, when students become recipients of professorial power plays in class, serve as pawns for a professor's pet research ideas and projects, and perhaps become targeted as the chosen ones to carry on an intellectual legacy. A teacher who stresses the importance of the intellectual virtues ought to desire something more than pedagogical cloning, epistemic chauvinism, and intellectual dishonesty.

The art of learning is an ongoing process that necessitates knowledge, truth, reasoning practices, humility, tenacity, curiosity, courage, discipline, patience, understanding, and wisdom. The result is a complex blend of knowledge and experience in a community of teachers and researchers. Without knowledge, understanding, and wisdom, students never learn to decipher key themes and insights from the assigned material and connect them with real-world experiences. Downloading large quantities of facts rarely empowers people either to cultivate critical skills of evaluation or to desire further study of the subject matter. More specifically, professors must model a critical process for reading texts, showing how people develop arguments and pursue crucial themes from a particular angle. Critical thinking, in this sense, is a skill that students must see and learn to embody as a community of inquirers.

In addition, the art of learning relates teaching and research to the question of what it means to be human. Skilled teachers and researchers are able to intertwine "a complex web of connections among themselves, their subjects, and their students so that [members of the community] can learn to weave a world for themselves" and to imagine one beyond their own as well.[30] Such activities carve out space for exploring issues in the company of others while seeking to expand horizons.[31] As Martha Nussbaum points out, the process of becoming an educated citizen means "learning how to be a human being capable of love and imagination." Producing "narrow citizens who have difficulty understanding people different from themselves" is foreign both to Nussbaum's notion of cultivating humanity and to my own constructive focus on the link between an integrative habit of mind and the pursuit of wisdom. Conversely, members within a community of inquirers, motivated by the goal of acquiring a connected view, extend their own self-awareness by considering—even incorporating—the insights of others. "By an increasingly refined exchange of both experience and argument," teachers and students "should gradually take on the ability to distinguish, within their own traditions, what is parochial from what may be commended as a norm for others, what is arbitrary and unjustified from that which may be justified by reasoned argument."[32]

Students can usually tell whether the professor understands teaching or research as a job or as a way of life. A set of different pedagogical and research qualities—such as the professor's passion for the subject matter, ongoing search for knowledge, humility, intellectual candor, knowledge of audience, apt communication skills, competence and awareness of current issues in the field, interest in student needs and perspectives, and the willingness to learn from others—will draw students into the learning process. Students remember the professor who humanizes the subject matter in their presence, displaying the intricacies, challenges, joy, and open-ended nature of learning. A posture of this sort invites students to examine the professorial struggle for and cultivation of knowledge, understanding, and wisdom while sharing in the learning process. In this sense, the professor stands before and with the students, embodying the "act of learning with a sort of honesty that we rarely encounter in everyday life."[33] In other words, embodied pedagogy forms and sustains a vibrant community of inquirers.

A community of inquirers, as we have seen, consists of people with various perspectives and from different disciplines. With this in mind, the art of learning requires us to discern how pedagogical strategies, the subject matter, and different learning styles form a proper fit. As Howard Gardner points out, for teaching to be effective, it is crucial to know the cognitive and pedagogical landscape of students. Teachers need "to be imaginative in selecting curricula, deciding how the curricula are to be taught or 'delivered,' and determining how student knowledge is to be demonstrated."[34] Pedagogical strategies of this sort require a vibrant community of inquirers. Engaging students in this way requires creative ways to meet teaching goals while relating ideas to the particular context of students. Thus, teachers and researchers strive to link new and existing knowledge in "spontaneous, improvised efforts of mind and spirit, disciplined by education and experience."[35] They discover how a connected view takes shape within a particular community of inquirers.

INTERDISCIPLINARITY AND THE PURSUIT OF WISDOM

The notion of a connected view has profound significance for our contemporary scene. People must embody "a special preparation of mind" to acquire skillful judgment in each "department of inquiry and discussion" (GA 321).[36] However, proficient reasoning, or cultivated judgment, in one area does not imply the same level in another. As we have seen, acquiring a connected view is socially and communally based; it is also not restricted to one area of inquiry. Along these lines, cultivating an interdisciplinary frame of mind is rarely a private matter or something that comes naturally. It usually takes place within a community of inquirers and requires a set of practices that enable cognitive agents to deal with different viewpoints. An emphasis of this sort challenges the impulse to insulate personal insights from the larger conversation. It begins with the noetic makeup of cognitive agents and then seeks to identify the relevant factors, materials, practices, and people that contribute toward broadening horizons.

It is easy to confuse the emphasis on forming a connected view in teachers and researchers with a kind of individualism or with mastery in one domain of inquiry. However, intimated in the notion of a connected view is the process of developing and embodying an interdisciplinary frame of mind:

> Personal independence of mind cannot be absolute, but only a relative independence, that is to say, such as will assure the individual person's freedom from unreliable and fictitious authorities and safeguard his own responsibilities for the control of his mind. It imposes on a man the duty to hearken to

what other men have to say, nay more, to study their ideas at first hand, but leaves him with the right to differ from them if he considers he must do so. The necessity which is incumbent on the philosopher to seek the truth in dialogue with other men is a metaphysical necessity, rooted in the limitations of every human mind: each person sees but an aspect of things he knows only in part. The richer an idea the more varied are the aspects under which it can be viewed. Thus the whole truth which the philosopher seeks can only become known if many minds work together and seek it with each other, with a mental respect for the authority due to the views of each investigator.[37]

The claim seems to be that "only after having pursued such a course of learning from recognized experts can the individual come to rely upon his own personal moral or intellectual judgment."[38] With this in mind, teachers and researchers acquire greater levels of understanding either by "mastering the principles of the subject matter in which the Quaestio lies, which is a work of time [informed judgment], or [by] availing [themselves] of the decisions of those who have mastered them [epistemic dependence]."[39] Thus, identifying reliable processes and fruitful conversation partners is crucial for making interdisciplinary connections. The desire to integrate new knowledge into previously accumulated knowledge necessitates the intersection of perspectives within a particular discipline and from different fields of knowledge.

Interdisciplinarity is indispensable for deciphering discipline-specific ways of thinking and reasoning across disciplines. Undergirding this requirement of understanding is a stable intellect, refined and enhanced by disciplined reflection and vibrant practices. Intellectual stability of this sort requires the presence of mind to see connections, thereby avoiding prematurely drawn connections and imperialistically applied principles and methods. When teachers and researchers shaped in this way come together, they refine their expertise and seek to connect themes, methodological concerns, and issues across the disciplines.[40] Through frequent exchanges they acquire a familiar sense of how things go and learn together how to fine-tune "the claims and relations of their respective subjects of investigation. They learn to respect, consult, [and] to aid each other" (*Idea* 76). Because of these collaborative practices, teachers and researchers form an interdisciplinary frame of mind that "lasts through life, of which the attributes are, freedom, equitableness, calmness, moderation, and wisdom" (*Idea* 76).

People formed in this way challenge surface conversations, ecclesial narrow-mindedness, and academic monologues. For example, the urge to latch on to a one-dimensional approach to religion—whether critically or uncritically—is close to what Newman describes as narrow-mindedness in the *University Sermons*. On the contrary, cultivating an integrative habit of mind, as I have argued, includes both objective and subjective conditions. The goal is not to "assign victory" to either subjective or objective conditions but to hold them "clearly in one's mind without suppressing either element."[41] The aim is to move beyond the way things appear to us, expand our understanding, and with such broadened horizons reject extreme and oversimplified accounts of the issue at hand.

The contemporary milieu of the university illustrates the challenges of pursuing wisdom and of navigating the murky waters of interdisciplinary teaching and research. In this regard, the twofold task is (1) to identify domain-specific procedures of investigation and (2) to make connections across the disciplines without blurring important distinctions. Undergirding an activity of this sort is "the perfection of the intellect" in which teachers and researchers "leaven the dense mass of facts" and render a "clear, calm, accurate vision and comprehension of all things" (*Idea* 104–105). Intellectual stability in this way promotes interdisciplinary knowledge, understanding, and wisdom.

Success is not a necessary condition to the process of forming an interdisciplinary frame of mind. Regardless of the outcome, it is right to be intellectually honest, it is important to pursue truth, and it is crucial to embody other intellectual virtues such as humility, understanding, and wisdom. Obviously, the focus remains the same; pursuing truth, knowledge, understanding, and wisdom is fundamental to epistemic well-being, but we recognize the fallibility of such a journey. Some examples come to mind here. People who are intellectually honest do not necessarily form true justified beliefs. Yet, normatively speaking, we see the value of intellectual honesty over intellectual dishonesty as a preferred way to regulate epistemic conduct. The fact that we readily praise intellectual giants such as Aristotle, Augustine, Aquinas, Newton, Galileo, Einstein, and so on, even though they all fall short of epistemic perfection, "is eloquent testimony to the fact that success at accomplishing the immediate targets of cognition or inquiry, true belief, is not necessary for intellectual virtue."[42]

Wisdom is a missing ingredient in the current talk about interdisciplinary teaching and research. First, the pursuit of wisdom is fundamental to a Newmanian vision of things and is, in my estimation, deeply relevant to the ongoing conversation about the nature, scope, and aims of the educational process. Second, teachers, researchers, and administrators ought to foster a learning environment that both resists academic cloning and empowers students to pursue truth, to evaluate arguments, to form their own conclusions, to see how things hang together, and so forth. Third, the pursuit of wisdom is not reserved only for teachers and researchers. Rather, space ought to be provided for all to participate in the shared pursuit of understanding and wisdom.

Instead of looking exclusively through one's own discipline-specific glasses, the subject matter becomes the mediator of dialogue. The former is hard to resist, given the pressure to establish one's own specialization and one's own research track record. Both of these aspirations are noble and right, though we need to rethink the conditions under which people acquire scholarly and pedagogical forms of excellence. This stems precisely from the fact that learning environments presume dynamic and communal processes in terms of how people acquire knowledge, understanding, and wisdom in different domains.

Mastering a specific field of knowledge does not necessarily preclude the praiseworthy desire to form an expansive intellect (a connected and more comprehensive view of things), nor does it necessarily generate epistemic occupiers and usurpers of academic turf. The goal is to connect discipline-specific forms of existing knowledge and see how they coalesce into a more comprehensive vision of things. As we have seen, the pursuit of wisdom (especially as it pertains to the goal of forming a connected view in researchers and teachers) "implies a connected view of the old with the new" (*US* 287). It nurtures conversation, creating the kind of intellectual environment in which "the paradigm of philosophical interaction is the quiet conversation of friends who have an intimate knowledge of one another's character and situation."[43]

Wisdom is not simply a wonderful—but impossible—ideal. Rather, embodiment turns idea into concrete reality. For example, a Newmanian-shaped philosophy of education calls to mind the Socratic way of being in the world. Such a posture suggests that books may remind us of vibrant modes of philosophical teaching, but they never replace philosophical activity. More specifically, books "do not themselves *do* philosophy." In fact, "they may actually impede that activity. For in one who reveres them, they may induce passivity and the 'false conceit of wisdom.'"[44]

Newman concurs that pedagogical exemplars instantiate the idea of a university, thereby fostering a vibrant place of learning and a healthy exchange of ideas. The university is not simply a place for students to download bits of information. Rather, it is a collaborative enterprise fleshed out in the communal existence of pedagogical and research exemplars. In other words, a connected view, as an important feature of integrative habit of mind, humanizes knowledge and holds that embodied wisdom is indispensable to university education.

Obviously, a Newmanian take on both philosophy and wisdom extends beyond current definitions and terminology. Most universities, for example, restrict the word "philosophy" to a department on campus with its varied specializations—logic, metaphysics, epistemology, ethics, philosophy of mind, philosophy of language, aesthetics, political philosophy, and so on. As we have seen, recent conversation about including understanding and wisdom on the list of desiderata indicates an interest in expanding the enterprise of epistemology.

In this regard, Pierre Hadot has persuasively argued that ancient philosophy and the subsequent traditions of Greco-Roman and Christian thought integrated philosophy and spirituality. They combined discourse and way of life. Spirituality was not merely an existential shot in the dark but a pursuit of discourse through concrete forms of philosophical *ascesis*. The goal was to live out what one deemed central through philosophical reflection.[45] Newman's affinity with the patristic notion of the context aspects of reasoning fits Hadot's narrative.

An interdisciplinary frame of mind, as intimated in the notion of a connected view, must be instantiated by professors and students on campus. Connecting disciplines while respecting the distinctions among them necessitates the cultivation of pedagogical and research exemplars of wisdom. Reductionism is counter-productive to this kind of interdisciplinarity. It excludes those that refuse to embrace narrow definitions of knowledge, thereby creating silos of learning and fostering a rationale of domain-specific entitlement.

A recent example is human selfhood. A topic of this sort demands contributions from various fields of knowledge, such as cognitive science, psychology, biology, philosophy, literature, and religion, yet the resurgence of logical positivism dressed up in the clothes of materialism gives birth to new forms of scientism. The collapse of collegial interaction creates suspicion, turf wars, and fragmented centers of higher learning. The tendency, for example, to naturalize everything speaks volumes. At the end of our contemporary day, the "self" from this narrow glance is an illusion, a thin collection of neurons created by biological processes, rather than a thickly populated agent.[46] The relevance of a constructive focus on wisdom, shaped by Newman's thought, lies in the critique of narrow approaches to complex and multifaceted phenomena. Wisdom is crucial for rethinking how various fields of knowledge may contribute to the kind of holistic learning that a Newmanian way of being envisions within the context of the university. An indispensable component of this kind of learning is the capacity to decipher relevant conversation partners for a particular topic.

Discerning an appropriate division of cognitive labor is what I have in mind here. Our fields of knowledge usually do not furnish processes and practices for grasping relevant connections. The move toward a comprehensive view of things calls for connections among the different fields of knowledge, not merely discipline-specific expertise. Paul Thagard, for example, argues that cognitive science is an interdisciplinary enterprise that draws insights from psychology, philosophy, anthropology, linguistics, neuroscience, and artificial intelligence. However, such a project needs to involve more than just different people meeting for lunch to chat about the mind. Before "we can begin to see the unifying ideas of cognitive science, we have to appreciate the diversity of outlooks and methods that researchers in different fields bring to the study of mind and intelligence."[47] The dynamic here, as most educators know, is complex, frightening, and exciting all at the same time. We use the language of interdisciplinary teaching, learning, and research, but we recognize in our own practices the immense gap between rhetoric and reality.

Consequently, those committed to an integrative habit of mind (especially as it relates to interdisciplinarity) must form and sustain a vibrant ethos in which people participate in and see firsthand the ongoing pursuits of truth, knowledge, understanding, and wisdom. If teachers, students, researchers, for example, value such pursuits as worthy goals, then they must conduct thorough inquiries, scrutinize evidence carefully, investigate numerous fields of study, consider alternative explanations, and consult other sources of wisdom. Such a desire ought to materialize in discerning whether belief-forming processes, practices, and people yield true beliefs over false ones, and whether these habits facilitate greater levels of understanding.

Newman's notion of a connected view, though reflective of his own context, is relevant for our environments of teaching and research. Obviously, contextual differences complicate an uncritical adoption of Newman's ideas, but both the processes of educating students and of engaging in research projects are still humanizing enterprises. Teachers and researchers make a difference in how students form, evaluate, and connect ideas. Both need to facilitate the cultivation of a connected view.

The practices of interdisciplinary learning and research, as intimated in this chapter, are an essential component of forming and sustaining a connected view within a community of inquirers. Both activities are not solo acts. Skillful assessment of salient pieces of data, issues, and insights "involves a subcommunity in interaction."[48] A community of inquirers recognizes both the enormous task of acquiring knowledge, understanding, and wisdom from various domains of inquiry and the importance of exhibiting epistemic humility in collaboration with others.

However, insisting on interdisciplinary teaching and research is not enough, especially since there is no ready-made consensus that currently holds together the various disciplines. It seems highly unlikely that "the many pressures towards becoming a set of largely separate institutes will be resisted unless there is a well thought-out and strongly articulated conception of the university to which interdisciplinarity is intrinsic."[49] With this challenge in mind, professorial modeling of interdisciplinary learning and research goes far with students (and hopefully with others), and perhaps this is a good place to start. If students detect from the professor an insulated approach to education, the results will generally be the same.

With the ever-growing realization of how expansive our knowledge and understanding are, the division of cognitive labor is imperative. The time for collaborative learning is also necessary simply because of the shift in how higher education is conceived. Students, along with faculty, both learn and interact with the world differently, embodying various learning styles and processing new ideas along these pedagogical lines. As we strive toward integration of domain-specific forms of inquiry, universities need to furnish contexts in which students can learn (1) to think critically and (2) to weave ideas from different sources of informed judgment into a coherent account. Such a move stresses the particularity of domain-specific modes of thinking, but it stretches students to make connections across disciplines.

I conclude this chapter with two concrete suggestions. First, team-teaching and collaborative research projects may be fruitful ways to enhance learning communities. Faculty from various disciplines should engage seriously in collaborative projects with the intent of discussing agreed-upon topics and learning from one another. One way is to bring together professors and students from different fields of knowledge in order to focus on a common theme. Second, university-wide committees need to support and nurture collaborative learning. Students need to see the internal logic of various disciplines across the curriculum, understanding the basic assumptions and rules of procedure of each discipline. An integrative habit of mind calls us to understand particular and distinct ways of proceeding. Wisdom is manifest in all—not merely some—disciplines of study and functions as an indispensable ingredient for cultivating the mind in rich, diverse, and coherent ways.

AFTERWORD

"We who plague people with words are many nowadays, while those who teach or are taught by actions are few."
—Maximus the Confessor, *Capita de caritate*

Undergirding the threefold focus of this book is an emphasis on the importance of cultivating and embodying an integrative habit of mind. I have drawn attention to the thick aspects of epistemic reflection and conduct and stressed the importance of moving from a particular set of claims to a more comprehensive understanding of the relevant matters at hand. A focus of this sort, for example, involves seeing the unreflective and reflective aspects of human cognition as a matter of proper fit. The motivation to understand how various pieces of data fit together in light of one another initiates and directs action toward achieving such an end (forming a connected view in teachers and researchers, for example). Thus, an integrative habit of mind does not entail an exaggerated claim of autonomy, nor does it involve an unhealthy appeal to authority; instead, broadening horizons is indispensable to the processes of acquiring greater levels of understanding and learning in order to make apt judgments in different contexts.

ROADBLOCKS?

Cultivating an integrative habit of mind is deeply relevant to our contemporary scene precisely in terms of mapping out the conditions and evaluative qualities requisite for regulating epistemic conduct and for expanding horizons. The transition from Newman's context to our own is complex, however, laden with philosophical, hermeneutical, and ecclesiastical dilemmas. Two options, for example, create roadblocks that hinder the formation and embodiment of an integrative habit of mind. On the one hand, the hagiographical option bypasses challenges of this sort, insulating Newman from rigorous historical and philosophical scrutiny. On the other hand, the hypercritical posture oversimplifies or misses the subtlety of Newman's thought and therefore relegates him to the status of a relic. From either angle, a constructive appropriation is nearly impossible.

My constructive proposal fits neither of these options. Rather, Robert Nozick's observation about the process of reading texts corresponds more with the way in which I have reconsidered Newman's thought as a conceptual point of departure for showing how the cultivation of an integrative habit of mind shapes the pursuit of wisdom:

> The author's voice is never our own, exactly; the author's life is never our own. It would be disconcerting, anyway, to find that another person holds precisely our views, responds with our particular sensibility, and thinks exactly the same things important. Still, we can gain from these books, weighing and pondering ourselves in their light. These books . . . invite or urge us to think along with them, branching in our own directions. We are not identical with the books we read, but neither would we be the same without them.[1]

Likewise, I am not suggesting that we ought to view Newman's thought as a repository of timeless truths. Nonetheless, I have argued that select features of an integrative habit of mind, embedded in Newman's thought, hold constructive promise under critical scrutiny.

With this in mind, the pursuit of wisdom lies not in making facile connections between the past and present but in seeking constructive possibilities, actualized by complementary insights. The historical lessons about connecting a figure's thought with contemporary issues are painful but necessary. In the aftermath of brilliant attempts to secure philosophical foundations of the Christian faith (as in the work of Aquinas, Descartes, Locke, Kant, Schleiermacher, and Rahner, for example),[2] perhaps we can glean some insights from Newman, a fallible voice of wisdom. However, it is problematic, to say the least, to assume that the transfer of Newman's thought to our own setting is rule-governed or equivalent to an uncritical download of isolated facts or truths. What we see in Newman is a perceptive grasp of profound truths in the height of skepticism, rationalism, and fideism. Thus, the move to our own context requires an imaginative lens, a posture of epistemic humility, and the capacity to recognize salient insights.

PURSUING WISDOM

The quotation from Maximus the Confessor above aptly captures a comparable and profound disconnect between words and actions in our contemporary world. Words alone or even desire alone will not endow a person with understanding or wisdom. In contrast, an integrative habit of mind requires a stable disposition, appropriate levels of training, disciplined reflection, the courage to engage and learn from a circle of interlocutors, and the ability to see how things fit together in light of one another. Accordingly, the pursuit of wisdom, undergirded by an integrative habit of mind, entails broadening horizons, rendering apt judgments, and forming a connected view.

People and communities that claim to be interested in acquiring wisdom need to promote and not obstruct the requisite avenues for acquiring a good of this sort. An integrative habit of mind is all about having the right state of mind and the evaluative qualities that enable cognitive agents to achieve such a desired end. In this regard, Terrence Tilley highlights an important though difficult challenge for seeing how the exercise of wisdom is related to the process of making or maintaining a commitment to moral and religious practices:

> We can see the complexity of the virtue *phronesis* both in 'morality' and 'religion.' The better religions promote and the worse ones obstruct those who dwell within them from acquiring that taste for Wisdom. The better religions allow the others to be different and to question those who dwell within them; the worse ones remake the image of the other to fit 'our' views and never allow 'them' to question 'our' terms. The better ones find room for difference even in the face of institutional authority, while the worse ones require everyone to walk lockstep or leave the tradition. . . . They constrict and destroy the discourse community and the traditions that can be brought into conversation.[3]

Tilley's observation very much pertains to our current context and set of challenges. A commitment to wisdom refuses to close off possibilities for acquiring a more expansive way of thinking. In the midst of complex issues and competing claims, we need exemplars of wisdom.

In this book, I have by no means fleshed out a full-blown theory of wisdom, nor have I furnished a comprehensive definition of wisdom. Rather, I have offered some suggestions about how an integrative habit of mind shapes the pursuit of wisdom. Another important ingredient in terms of the constructive task ahead of us involves seeing how the pursuit of wisdom, grounded in and shaped by an integrative habit of mind, takes up the problem of testimonial injustice (as in the refusal to hear people out, especially in light of biases and prejudices).[4] People that desire to instantiate an integrative habit of mind must make every effort to avoid undermining others; in so doing they may avoid missing out on the wisdom offered.[5] We know what happens when people are unwilling to open up their own views to critical reflection—and when they refuse to glean insights from others.

An integrative habit of mind hones in on a regulative approach to the pursuit of wisdom. It seeks to link different forms of inquiry. In an expansionist manner, the notion here is not to pit a belief-based approach to wisdom against one that is agent-based. Rather, the key is to see the extent to which different evaluative ends require a different set of tools and aims.[6] It is my hope that the focus of this book will provoke further reflection and development toward this end.

Notes

INTRODUCTION

1. Catherine Elgin, *Considered Judgment* (Princeton, NJ: Princeton University Press, 1996), 106. For further reflection on the notion of informed judgment, see Frederick D. Aquino, *Communities of Informed Judgment: Newman and Accounts of Rationality* (Washington, DC: Catholic University of America Press, 2004).

2. Michael Walzer, *Thick and Thin: Moral Argument at Home and Abroad* (Notre Dame, IN: University of Notre Dame Press, 1997), 98. See also Stanley Cavell, *Cities of Words: Pedagogical Letters on a Register of the Moral Life* (Cambridge, MA: The Belknap Press of Harvard University Press, 2004).

3. Charles Taylor, *Sources of the Self: The Making of the Modern Identity* (Cambridge, MA: Harvard University Press, 1989), 27. For further reflection on the different publics of theological reflection and how they intersect, see David Tracy, *The Analogical Imagination: Christian Theology and the Culture of Pluralism* (New York: Crossroad, 1981).

4. See John McDowell, *The Engaged Intellect: Philosophical Essays* (Cambridge, MA: Harvard University Press, 2009).

5. On this distinction in philosophy of science, see Eric Christian Barnes, *The Paradox of Predictivism* (Cambridge: Cambridge University Press, 2008).

6. Sanford Goldberg, *Anti-individualism: Mind and Language, Knowledge and Justification* (Cambridge: Cambridge University Press, 2007), 135.

7. Terrence Tilley, *The Wisdom of Religious Commitment* (Washington, DC: Georgetown University Press, 1995), 133.

8. Martha Nussbaum, *Love's Knowledge: Essays on Philosophy and Literature* (New York: Oxford University Press, 1990), 25.

9. For further reflection, see Walzer, *Thick and Thin*; Guy Axtell and J. Adam Carter, "Just the Right Thickness: A Defense of Second-Wave Virtue Epistemology," *Philosophical Papers* 37 (2008): 413–434.

10. In *The Idea of a University*, ed. Martin J. Svaglic (Notre Dame, IN: University of Notre Dame Press, 1982), henceforth cited as *Idea*, for example, Newman develops and applies his conception of the philosophical habit of mind to the context of university education, and in the *Grammar of Assent*, he unpacks and shows the significance of the illative sense for constructing an epistemology of religious belief.

11. In *Idea*, XLIII, Newman says the goal of training and forming the intellect is to acquire "a connected view or grasp of things." In *Fifteen Sermons Preached before the University of Oxford*, intro. Mary Katherine Tillman (Notre Dame, IN: University of Notre Dame Press, 1997), henceforth cited as *US*, 279, Newman refers to wisdom as the "orderly and mature development of thought,"

"an enlargement or expansion of mind," and a "comprehensive view of things." In *An Essay in Aid of a Grammar of Assent*, intro. Nicholas Lash (Notre Dame, IN: University of Notre Dame Press, 1979), henceforth cited as *GA*, 160, 271, Newman speaks of perfecting or cultivating the illative sense or "mature judgment."

12. Tilley alludes to the many faces of the virtue of wisdom. Wisdom clearly is a virtue, yet "Aristotle called it *phronesis*; St. Thomas Aquinas designated it *prudentia*; John Henry Newman wrote of an 'illative sense'" (*Wisdom of Religious Commitment*, 3).

13. William Alston says that some aspects of the cognitive side of human life, from an epistemic point of view, include "the operation and condition of our cognitive faculties—perception, reasoning, belief formation: the products thereof—beliefs, theories, explanations, knowledge; and the evaluation of all that." Moreover, "putting intellectual virtues into the picture will involve adding epistemic *subjects, cognitive agents, persons* to the list of targets of epistemic evaluation" (*Beyond Justification: Dimensions of Epistemic Evaluation* [Ithaca, NY: Cornell University Press, 2005]), 2–4. On the social dimension of epistemology, see Alvin Goldman, *Knowledge in a Social World* (Oxford: Clarendon Press, 1999); Frederick Schmitt, ed., *Socializing Epistemology: The Social Dimensions of Knowledge* (Lanham, MD: Rowman and Littlefield, 1994); Tamar Szabó Gendler and John Hawthorne, eds., *Oxford Studies in Epistemology* (Oxford: Oxford University Press, 2010), vol. 3, especially chapters 8–13.

14. Jonathan Kvanvig, "Truth Is not the Primary Epistemic Goal," in *Contemporary Debates in Epistemology*, ed. Matthias Steup and Ernest Sosa (Oxford: Blackwell, 2005), 286; see also Paul Moser, *Philosophy after Objectivity: Making Sense in Perspective* (Oxford: Oxford University Press, 1993), 176–177.

15. For helpful discussion of epistemic value monism and epistemic value pluralism, see Kvanvig, "Truth Is not the Primary Epistemic Goal," 285–296; Jonathan Kvanvig, *The Value of Knowledge and the Pursuit of Understanding* (New York: Cambridge University Press, 2003); Alston, *Beyond Justification*; William Alston, "Epistemic Desiderata," *Philosophy and Phenomenological Research* 53 (1993): 527–551; Robert Roberts and Jay Wood, *Intellectual Virtues: An Essay in Regulative Epistemology* (Oxford: Clarendon Press, 2007); Wayne Riggs, "Understanding 'Virtue' and the Virtue of Understanding," in Michael DePaul and Linda Zagzebski, eds., *Intellectual Virtue: Perspectives from Ethics and Epistemology* (Oxford: Clarendon Press, 2003), 203–226; Wayne Riggs, "The Value Turn in Epistemology," in *New Waves in Epistemology*, ed. Vincent F. Hendricks and Duncan Pritchard (New York: Palgrave Macmillan, 2008), 300–323; Moser, *Philosophy after Objectivity*, esp. chapter 4; Richard Foley, "Conceptual Diversity in Epistemology," in *Contemporary Debates in Epistemology*, ed. Matthias Steup and Ernest Sosa (Oxford: Blackwell, 2005), 177–203; Duncan Pritchard, "Recent Work on Epistemic Value," *American Philosophical Quarterly* 44 (2007): 85–110; John Greco, *Achieving Knowledge: A Virtue-Theoretic Account of Epistemic Normativity* (Cambridge: Cambridge University Press, 2010), esp. chapter 1.

16. Tilley, *Wisdom of Religious Commitment*, 6.

17. Alston says that the "most striking implication of this diversity is the fact that in everyday life there seems to be no single desideratum or set of desiderata that are epistemically crucial in all contexts." However, Alston restricts the focus here to the status of beliefs. Moreover, he argues that the primary function in human life, from an epistemic point of view, is "to acquire true rather than false beliefs about matters that are of interest or of importance to us" (*Beyond Justification*, 176, 29).

18. See, for example, Joseph Dunne, *Back to the Rough Ground: Practical Judgment and the Lure of Technique* (Notre Dame, IN: University of Notre Dame Press, 1992). Dunne's larger project is to employ Newman and others (e.g., R. G. Collingwood, Hannah Arendt, Hans Georg Gadamer, Jurgen Habermas) to show the limitations of technical reason while providing a rationale for retrieving an Aristotelian account of phronesis. Since Dunne's proposal is primarily comparative in nature, it does not address fully Newman's account of the various aspects of the illative sense, nor does it show how his notions of a connected view in *The Idea of a University*, cultivated judgment in the *Grammar of Assent*, and wisdom in the *University Sermons* fit together in light of one another. Mark Wynn, *Emotional Experience and Religious Understanding: Integrating Perception, Conception and Feeling* (Cambridge: Cambridge University Press, 2005). Wynn approaches the landscape of philosophical theology from a reconceived theory of emotion. The options are not simply objective content over emotional form or vice versa. Wynn draws insights from thinkers such as McDowell, Newman, Alston, and Gaita to explain the role of emotions in acquiring understanding (value perception), though he does not develop Newman's account of understanding and wisdom. Thomas K. Carr, *Newman and Gadamer: Toward a Hermeneutics of Religious Knowledge* (Atlanta, GA: Scholars Press, 1996). Carr examines and compares the religious epistemology of John Henry Newman and the philosophical hermeneutics of Hans-Georg Gadamer, highlighting their common ground and their common mistakes. Carr offers a constructive aesthetics of knowing, but he fails to develop (though he does allude to) Newman's notion of personal judgment into communal forms of judgment and adjudication.

19. Alvin Goldman, *Epistemology and Cognition* (Cambridge, MA: Harvard University Press, 1986), 25. See also Alvin Plantinga, *Warrant: The Current Debate* (New York: Oxford University Press, 1993), 3–29.

20. Goldman, *Epistemology and Cognition*, 25.

21. Mary Katherine Tillman argues that the "*phronesis* tradition" provides "one of the best clues overall to John Henry Newman's view of the economizing activity of human reason." "Economies of Reason: Newman and the Phronesis Tradition," in *Discourse and Context: An Interdisciplinary Study of John Henry Newman*, ed. Gerard Magill (Carbondale: Southern Illinois University Press, 1993), 45.

22. See Terrence Merrigan, *Clear Heads and Holy Hearts: The Religious and Theological Ideal of John Henry Newman* (Louvain: Peeters Press, 1991).

23. Perhaps a helpful way to navigate the potential problem here is to see Newman in terms of the contemporary epistemological distinction between particularism and methodism. For further reflection on the distinction between particularism and methodism, see Roderick M. Chisholm, *The Problem of the Criterion* (Milwaukee: Marquette University Press, 1973). Newman's epistemological insights about acquiring a connected view fall under the category of particularism.

24. On this point, see John T. Ford, "Recent Studies on Newman: Two Review Articles," *The Thomist* 41 (1977): 424–440. Carr astutely notes a basic division of labor within Newman studies. There are those who tackle philosophical and theological issues on the one hand while there are those who look at Newman's "literary art, poetry, and rhetoric on the other" (*Newman and Gadamer*, 1). Though I do not intend to get into this issue, I would add that interpreters tend to divide the former categories into philosophical, theological, and ecclesiastical. I focus primarily on the philosophical component of Newman's thought.

25. Some notable exceptions, though they are still largely descriptive in nature, are Wilfrid Ward, *Last Lectures* (London: Longman's Green, 1918); Maurice Nédoncelle, *La Philosophie religieuse de John Henry Newman* (Strasburg, 1946); A. J. Boekraad, *Personal Quest of Truth* (Louvain: Nauwelaerts, 1955); A. J. Boekraad, *The Argument from Conscience to the Existence of God according to J. H. Newman* (Louvain: Nauwelaarts, 1961); and David A. Pailin, *The Way to Faith: An Examination of Newman's* Grammar of Assent *as a Response to the Search for Certainty in Faith* (London: Epworth Press, 1969).

26. J. M. Cameron rightly claims, "Newman's *philosophical* originality has been underestimated" ("Newman and Empiricism," *The Night Battle* [London: Burns and Oates, 1962], 223). In the introduction to the Notre Dame (1979) publication of the *Grammar of Assent*, Nicholas Lash argues that, for such "underestimation to be corrected, certain widespread assumptions concerning what is to count as philosophical argument in general, and, in particular as argument in the philosophy of religion, had first to be called into question." Lash adds that some fundamental shifts can be seen in recent assessments "of the range and variety of modes of human rationality" (*GA* 20). In my estimation, the fundamental shifts intimated by Lash can be seen in the constructive projects listed below in footnotes 27–38.

27. See M. Jamie Ferreira, *Doubt and Religious Commitment: The Role of the Will in Newman's Thought* (Oxford: Clarendon Press, 1980).

28. See Aquino, *Communities of Informed Judgment*.

29. Terrence Merrigan, "Newman and Theological Liberalism," *Theological Studies* 66 (2005): 621, 605.

30. Basil Mitchell, *The Justification of Religious Belief* (New York: Seabury Press, 1973); "Newman as a Philosopher," in *Newman after a Hundred Years*, ed. Ian T. Ker and Alan G. Hill (Oxford: Clarendon Press, 1990), 223–246; and *Faith and Criticism* (Oxford: Clarendon Press, 1994).

31. Ferreira, *Doubt and Religious Commitment*; M. Jamie Ferreira, *Scepti-*

cism and Reasonable Doubt: The British Naturalist Tradition in Wilkins, Hume, Reid and Newman (Oxford: Clarendon Press, 1986).

32. William Wainwright, *Reason and the Heart: A Prolegomenon to a Critique of Passional Reason* (Ithaca, NY: Cornell University Press, 1995).

33. Dunne, *Back to the Rough Ground.*

34. Martin Moleski, *Personal Catholicism: The Theological Epistemologies of John Henry Newman and Michael Polanyi* (Washington, DC: Catholic University of America Press, 2000). See also Andrew Louth, *Discerning the Mystery: An Essay on the Nature of Theology* (Oxford: Clarendon Press, 1990).

35. William Abraham, *Canon and Criterion in Christian Theology: From the Fathers to Feminism* (Oxford: Clarendon Press, 1998); William Abraham, *Crossing the Threshold of Divine Revelation* (Grand Rapids, MI: Eerdmans, 2006).

36. Aquino, *Communities of Informed Judgment*; "Broadening Horizons: Constructing an Epistemology of Religious Belief," *Louvain Studies* 30.3 (2005): 198–213; and "Externalism and Internalism: A Newmanian Matter of Proper Fit," *Heythrop Journal* 51 (2010): 1023–1034.

37. Wynn, *Emotional Experience and Religious Understanding.*

38. Carr, *Newman and Gadamer.*

1—BROADENING HORIZONS

1. Wilfrid P. Ward, *The Life of John Henry Cardinal Newman Based on His Private Journals and Correspondence*, 2 vols. (New York: Longmans, Green and Co., 1912), 2:266. As Ward points out, Newman's "aim was simply to rouse in men's minds certain perceptions as to their mental processes, rooted in the experience of mankind, but dormant, or apt to be dormant, because their practical importance is not directly obvious. And he trusted that these perceptions, once properly roused, would account for and justify important beliefs which could not adequately be proved by explicit logical arguments" (ibid.).

2. Ibid., 2:270–271.

3. For an excellent and critical study of Newman's use of Patristic writers, see Benjamin J. King, *Newman and the Alexandrian Fathers: Shaping Doctrine in Nineteenth-Century England* (Oxford: Clarendon Press, 2009).

4. Tracy adds: "The classic Ambrosian line 'Non in dialectica complacuit Deo salvum facere populum suum' determines the ethos and persuasive power of Newman's *The Grammar of Assent.* . . . Indeed an analysis of Newman's project in the *Grammar* in the light of the present distinctions among dialectics, rhetoric-poetics and ethics-politics would perhaps prove a more enlightening setting than one more round of the W.C. Clifford-William James debate on the 'will to believe'" (*The Analogical Imagination*, 86n33). See also Gerard Magill, "Newman's Personal Reasoning: The Inspiration of the Early Church," *Irish Theological Quarterly* 58 (1992): 304–313.

5. John L. Pollock argues, "Much work in epistemology falls short of producing rules for rational cognition. Accounts of how to reason inductively, or how

to reason about times and causes, or how to form beliefs on the basis of perceptual input, are not themselves complete rules of rationality. At best, they describe the rules the cognizer should follow in the absence of reflexive cognition. They are 'default rules' for how to cognize, but a complete account of rational cognition must not only describe these rules, but also explain how they fit into the more comprehensive architecture for rational cognition that characterizes both how we should reason in the absence of reflexive cognition and also how we should reason and perhaps violate some of these default rules in the course of reflexive cognition." "Irrationality and Cognition," in *Epistemology: New Essays*, ed. Quentin Smith (Oxford: Oxford University Press, 2008), 269–270.

6. John Henry Newman, *Letters and Diaries of John Henry Newman*, ed. Charles S. Dessain et al. (Oxford: Clarendon Press, 1976), henceforth cited as *L&D*, 29:106. Newman adds, "indeed this is one of the 'morals' of my Essay on Assent" (ibid.).

7. Terrence Merrigan, "Christianity and the Non-Christian Religions in the Light of the Theology of John Henry Newman," *Irish Theological Quarterly* 68 (2003): 346; see also Wynn, *Emotional Experience and Religious Understanding*. For an excellent exposition of the holistic nature of intellectual formation in early Christianity, see Robert L. Wilken, "Alexandria: A School for Training in Virtue," in *Schools of Thought in the Christian Tradition*, ed. Patrick Henry (Philadelphia: Fortress Press, 1984), 15–30.

8. Nussbaum, *Love's Knowledge*, 44.

9. John Henry Newman, *Apologia pro Vita Sua*, ed. David J. DeLaura (New York: W. W. Norton, 1968), henceforth cited as *Apo*, 222–223.

10. Richard Whately, *Elements of Logic*, 9th ed. (Boston: James Monroe and Co., 1858; henceforth cited as *EL*), xix. In this regard, logical argument is "the most important intellectual occupation of Man" (ibid., xix). As William R. Fey points out: "While the Enlightenment had driven many continental Christian intellectuals into fideism or sentimentalism, it tended to advance the trend in the Church of England toward a rationalization of Christianity into those doctrines which would survive the strictest logical tests. The Noetics argued that no one has a right to believe until he has applied to his claims the same canons used by mathematicians and physicists." The assumption here is that when logic, as the most appropriate intellectual occupation of humans, "is obtained it compels assent to the articles of Christian belief. But by establishing a proportion between the reasonableness of one's beliefs and the rigour of objective proof, this school tended to reserve a well-founded faith for the scholarly few who could master technical proofs." William R. Fey, *Faith and Doubt: The Unfolding of Newman's Thought on Certainty* (Shepherdstown, WV: Patmos Press, 1976), 1.

11. Whately adds: "The rules already given enable us to develop the principles on which all reasoning is conducted, whatever be the Subject-matter of it, and to ascertain the validity of fallaciousness of any apparent argument, as far as the *form of expression* is concerned; that being alone the proper province of Logic" (*EL* 171).

12. Terrence Merrigan, "Newman's Oriel Experience: Its Significance for His Life and Thought," *Bijdragen* 47 (1986): 193.

13. For a comparative treatment of tacit knowledge in Newman and Polanyi, see Moleski, *Personal Catholicism.*

14. Roberts and Wood, *Intellectual Virtues,* offer a helpful commentary on the antecedent traditions of regulative epistemology—in Descartes and in Locke, for example. More importantly, they show the relevance of this kind of emphasis for contemporary epistemology.

15. In a letter to Whately, Newman reiterates the point: "Much as I owe to Oriel in the way of mental improvement, to none, as I think, do I owe so much as to you. I know who it was that first gave me heart to look about me after my election and taught me to think correctly, and (strange office for an instructor) to rely upon myself." John Henry Newman, *Autobiographical Writings,* ed. Henry Tristam (New York: Sheed and Ward, 1957), 67–68.

16. In the preface, Whately gives Newman credit: "But I cannot avoid particularizing the Rev. J. Newman, Fellow of Oriel College, who actually composed a considerable portion of the work as it now stands, from manuscripts not designed for publication, and who is the original author of several pages" (*EL* xv).

17. For example, see Sermons 13 and 14 in *US* and chapters 6–9 in *GA.*

18. Gerard Magill, "Introduction: The Intellectual Ethos of John Henry Newman," in *Discourse and Context: An Interdisciplinary Study of John Henry Newman,* ed. Gerard Magill (Carbondale: Southern Illinois University Press, 1993), 4.

19. Nussbaum, *Love's Knowledge,* 38.

20. In a letter to William Froude, Newman states, "Nothing surely have I insisted on more earnestly in my Essay on Assent, than on the necessity of thoroughly subjecting abstract propositions to the concrete. It is in the experience of daily life that the power of religion is learnt. . . . And I repeat, it is not by syllogisms or other logical process that trustworthy conclusions are drawn, such as command our assent, but by that minute, continuous, experimental reasoning, which shows baldly on paper, but which drifts silently into an overwhelming cumulus of proof, and, when our start is true, brings us on to a true result." Gordon H. Harper, ed., *Cardinal Newman and William Froude, FRS: A Correspondence* (Baltimore: Johns Hopkins Press, 1933), 204.

21. For a fascinating treatment of the normative and descriptive aspects of human cognition, see Pollock, "Irrationality and Cognition," 249–275.

22. In *Problems of Knowledge: A Critical Introduction to Epistemology* (Oxford: Oxford University Press, 2001), 32, Michael Williams makes a Newmanian kind of observation: "Of course, we can try to think up justifications as 'rational reconstructions' of unreflectively held views [e.g., that we inhabit an external world not of our own making], but to what end? Such rationalizations will amount only to 'arguments on paper.'"

23. As Pollock points out, humans "have a built-in cognitive module that enables them rapidly to predict trajectories on the basis of visual information.

At a higher level, explicit inductive or probabilistic reasoning imposes a tremendous cognitive load on the cognizer. We avoid that by using various [quick and inflexible] modules that summarize data as we accumulate it, without forcing us to recall all the data, and then makes generalizations on the basis of the summary" ("Irrationality and Cognition," 254).

24. Paul Moser rightly points out that, in seeking to make sense of divine matters (the nature of God, for example), "we reach a point where explanation runs out, where ontology outstrips available explanation. . . . Mystery does indeed dog theism, and perhaps God, too. Still, not all explanation is lost, and mystery need not be a cause for lament in the end. *Ultimate* existence may reside where explanation runs out and mystery flourishes." *The Elusive God: Reorienting Religious Epistemology* (Cambridge: Cambridge University Press, 2008), 89.

25. See Thomas Vargish, *Newman: The Contemplation of Mind* (Oxford: Clarendon Press, 1970).

26. On the principle of credulity, see William Alston, *Perceiving God: The Epistemology of Religious Experience* (Ithaca, NY: Cornell University Press, 1991); Richard Swinburne, *Epistemic Justification* (Oxford: Clarendon Press, 2001); or on what some call the principle of phenomenal conservatism (PC), see Michael Huemer, *Skepticism and the Veil of Perception* (Lanham, MD: Rowman and Littlefield, 2001). Huemer states PC in the following way: "If it seems to S as if P, then S thereby has at least prima facie justification for believing that P" (*Skepticism*, 99).

27. On this point, see Aquino, *Communities of Informed Judgment*, especially chapter 4.

28. Newman takes up the issue of dogmatism, enthusiasm, superstition, and narrow-mindedness in "Love the Safeguard of Faith against Superstition" (*US* 13) and "Wisdom, as Contrasted with Faith and Bigotry" (*US* 14).

29. John Henry Newman, *The Theological Papers of John Henry Newman on Faith and Certainty*, ed. Hugo M. de Achaval and J. Derek Holmes (Oxford: Clarendon Press, 1976), 102.

30. On this point, see Nicholas Lash, *The Beginning and the End of Religion* (Cambridge: Cambridge University Press, 1996), 58.

31. See, for example, Abraham, *Canon and Criterion*; Ellen T. Charry, *By the Renewing of Your Minds: The Pastoral Function of Christian Doctrine* (Oxford: Oxford University Press, 1997); Sarah Coakley, *Powers and Submissions: Spirituality, Gender, and Philosophy* (Oxford: Blackwell, 2002).

32. John Coulson, "Newman's Hour: The Significance of Newman's Thought, and Its Application Today," *Heythrop Journal* 22 (1981): 402.

33. Pierre Hadot, *What Is Ancient Philosophy?* trans. Michael Chase (Cambridge, MA: The Belknap Press of Harvard University Press, 2002), 274.

34. See sermon 14 in *US* and a fuller conception in *The Idea of a University*.

35. Pierre Hadot, *Philosophy as a Way of Life: Spiritual Exercises from Socrates to Foucault* (Oxford: Blackwell, 1995), 277, 279.

36. Williams, *Problems of Knowledge*, 8. See also Hadot, *Philosophy as a*

Way of Life; Bernard Williams, *Shame and Necessity* (Berkeley and Los Angeles: University of California Press, 1985); Bernard Williams, *Ethics and the Limits of Philosophy* (Cambridge, MA: Harvard University Press, 1993); Robert Solomon, *The Joy of Philosophy: Thinking Thin versus the Passionate Life* (New York: Oxford University Press, 1999).

37. Nussbaum, *Love's Knowledge*, 20.

38. Thomas Nagel, *Equality and Impartiality* (New York: Oxford University Press, 1991), 14, aptly describes the juxtaposition of standpoints (partial and impartial) in terms of "a division of the self." Quick resolutions of this tension simply exacerbate the problem.

39. On this point, see Roberts and Wood, *Intellectual Virtues*, especially chapter 1.

40. Julia Annas, *The Morality of Happiness* (New York: Oxford University Press, 1993), 52.

41. See Aquino, *Communities of Informed Judgment*, especially chapters 3 and 4.

42. See Jeffrey Stout, *Democracy and Tradition* (Princeton, NJ: Princeton University Press, 2004); Robert Audi, *Religious Commitment and Secular Reason* (Cambridge: Cambridge University Press, 2000); Martha Nussbaum, *Liberty of Conscience: In Defense of America's Tradition of Religious Equality* (New York: Basic Books, 2008); Christopher Eberle, *Religious Conviction in Liberal Politics* (Cambridge: Cambridge University Press, 2002); Mark Lilla, *The Stillborn God: Religion, Politics, and the Modern West* (New York: Vintage, 2007); Kent Greenawalt, *Religious Conviction and Political Choice* (Oxford: Oxford University Press, 1988); Charles Mathewes, *A Theology of Public Life* (Cambridge: Cambridge University Press, 2008); William Connolly, *Capitalism and Christianity, American Style* (Durham, NC: Duke University Press, 2008).

43. Jonathan Glover, *Humanity: A Moral History of the Twentieth Century* (New Haven: Yale University Press, 1999), 6. Glover provides an eye-opening account of humanity in the twentieth century. He offers a chastened but deeply committed project of the Enlightenment, a moral history of the human situation. In fact, Glover tries to "replace the thin, mechanical psychology of the Enlightenment with something more complex, something closer to reality." An additional aim "is to defend the Enlightenment hope of a world that is more peaceful and more humane, the hope that by understanding more about ourselves we can do something to create a world with less misery" (ibid., 7).

44. See Taylor, *Sources of the Self*.

45. Jeffrey Stout, *The Flight from Authority: Religion, Morality, and the Quest for Autonomy* (Notre Dame, IN: University of Notre Dame Press, 1981), 37.

46. For a helpful treatment of how to rethink the public intersection of religion and politics, see Stout, *Democracy and Tradition*.

47. See Aquino, *Communities of Informed Judgment*, especially chapter 4.

48. See Joseph Raz, *Engaging Reason: On the Theory of Value and Action*

(Oxford: Oxford University Press, 1999); Joseph Raz, *Value, Respect, and Attachment* (Cambridge: Cambridge University Press, 2001); Walzer, *Thick and Thin*; Thomas Nagel, *The View from Nowhere* (Oxford: Oxford University Press, 1989); Nagel, *Equality and Impartiality*.

49. See Coakley, *Powers and Submissions*; Hadot, *Philosophy as a Way of Life*; John Cottingham, *The Spiritual Dimension: Religion, Philosophy and Value* (Cambridge: Cambridge University Press, 2005); Mark McIntosh, *Mystical Theology: The Integrity of Spirituality and Theology* (Oxford: Blackwell, 1998); Harriet A. Harris, "Does Analytical Philosophy Clip Our Wings? Reformed Epistemology as a Test Case," in *Faith and Philosophical Analysis: The Impact of Analytical Philosophy of Religion on the Philosophy of Religion*, ed. Harriet A. Harris and Christopher J. Insole (Aldershot: Ashgate, 2005), 100–118.

50. Roberts and Wood, *Intellectual Virtues*, 324.

51. Ibid., 21–22. See also Nicholas Wolterstorff, *John Locke and the Ethics of Belief* (Cambridge: Cambridge University Press, 1996).

52. Roberts and Wood, *Intellectual Virtues*, 21.

53. Ibid., 323, 27.

54. Richard Foley, "Egoism in Epistemology," in Schmitt, *Socializing Epistemology*, 72. For further reflection on the nature of our epistemic reliance on others, see Sanford C. Goldberg, *Relying on Others: An Essay in Epistemology* (Oxford: Oxford University Press, 2010).

55. Roberts and Wood, *Intellectual Virtues*, 281.

56. Kvanvig, *Value of Knowledge*, 192; see also Riggs, "Understanding 'Virtue,'" 203–226.

57. Goldman, *Knowledge in a Social World*. As Frederick F. Schmitt points out, a contemporary question in epistemology is "whether, and to what extent, the conditions of knowledge include social conditions. Is knowledge a property of knowers in isolation from their social setting (and in what sense of 'isolation'), or does it involve a relation between knowers and their social circumstances?" Schmitt, "Social Epistemology," in *The Blackwell Guide to Epistemology*, ed. John Greco and Ernest Sosa (Oxford: Blackwell Publishers, 1999), 354. For further consideration, see Schmitt, *Socializing Epistemology*.

58. For a fuller discussion about the relationship between the ontology of Christian identity and epistemic reflection, see William J. Abraham, Jason E. Vickers, and Natalie Van Kirk, eds., *Canonical Theism: A Proposal for Theology and the Church* (Grand Rapids, MI: Eerdmans, 2008).

59. For reliabilist versions of epistemology, see Goldman, *Epistemology and Cognition*; Fred Dretske, *Knowledge and the Flow of Information* (Cambridge, MA: MIT Press, 1981); Ernest Sosa, *Knowledge in Perspective: Selected Essays in Epistemology* (Cambridge: Cambridge University Press, 1991); John Greco, *Putting Skeptics in Their Place: The Nature of Skeptical Arguments and Their Role in Philosophical Inquiry* (Cambridge: Cambridge University Press, 2000). For cognitive science, see Gerd Gigerenzer, Peter M. Todd, and the ABC Research Group,

Simple Heuristics That Make Us Smart (New York: Oxford University Press, 1999); Timothy D. Wilson, *Strangers to Ourselves: Discovering the Adaptive Unconscious* (Cambridge, MA: The Belknap Press of Harvard University Press, 2002); Gilles Fauconnier and Mark Turner, *The Way We Think: Conceptual Blending and the Mind's Hidden Complexities* (New York: Basic Books, 2002); Ran R. Hassin, James S. Uleman, and John A. Bargh, eds., *The New Unconscious* (New York: Oxford University Press, 2005).

2—A MATTER OF PROPER FIT

1. As William P. Alston points out, those who wield the distinction between internalism and externalism "intend to be contrasting different views on what can confer justification or on what can convert mere true belief into knowledge. The main emphasis has been on justification. . . . In all these discussions it is the internalist position that lays down constraints; the externalist position vis-à-vis a given internalist position is simply the denial that the internalist constraint in question constitutes a necessary condition of justification." Alston, *Epistemic Justification: Essays in the Theory of Knowledge* (Ithaca, NY: Cornell University Press, 1989), 185.

2. As Sosa points out, there may be "justification-making properties of a belief which the believer could not possibly discover merely by reflection (introspection, memory, reason)." *Knowledge in Perspective*, 193.

3. Michael Bergmann argues that all versions of internalism have in common the requirement that "the person holding the belief be aware (or at least potentially aware) of something contributing to its justification." For example, "S's belief B is justified only if (i) there is something, X, that contributes to the justification of B—e.g. evidence for B or a truth indicator for B or the satisfaction of some necessary condition of B's justification—and (ii) S is aware (or potentially aware) of X." The internalist claim, according to Bergmann, is that "if you are aware of the justification-contributor, then it isn't an accident from your perspective that your belief is true; but if you are aren't aware of the justification-contributor, it *is* an accident from your perspective that your belief is true; and that difference (between its being an accident and its not being an accident) makes a difference in the justification of your belief." Michael Bergmann, *Justification without Awareness: A Defense of Epistemic Externalism* (Oxford: Clarendon Press, 2006), 9, 12. See also Alston, *Epistemic Justification*, especially essays 8 and 9; Alvin Goldman, *Pathways to Knowledge: Private and Public* (Oxford: Oxford University Press, 2002), especially chapter 1.

4. On the distinction between the state of being justified and the activity of justifying a belief, see Alston, *Perceiving God*, especially chapter 2. As Alston points out, "many persons are justified in many beliefs without possessing the intellectual or verbal skills to exhibit what justifies those beliefs. Thus, the *fact* of being justified is not dependent on any particular actual or possible activity of justifying" (*Epistemic Justification*, 236). In terms of the adequacy of the grounds

of the belief that *p*, Alston concludes that in order for a person's belief that *p*, which is based on ground G, "to be justified, it is quite sufficient, as well as necessary, that G be indicative of the truth of *p*." Yet, it is in no way required that one "know anything, or be justified in believing anything, about this relationship. No doubt, we sometimes do have justified beliefs about the adequacy of our grounds, and that it is certainly a good thing. But that is icing on the cake" (*Epistemic Justification*, 243–244). I want to make a similar move in terms of thinking about what is involved in the tacit and cultivated forms of judgment, especially as they relate to this feature of an integrative habit of mind. For an approach that aims at a better integration of the property and process aspects of justification, see Robert Audi, *The Structure of Justification* (Cambridge: Cambridge University Press, 1993).

5. Plantinga argues that the "notion of internality is fundamentally *epistemic*. Warrant and the properties that confer it are internal in that they are states or conditions of which the cognizer is or can be *aware*; they are states of which he has or can easily have knowledge; they are states or properties to which he has cognitive or epistemic access. . . . So the relevant sense of 'internal' is strongly epistemic; the internalist holds that a person has some kind of special epistemic access to warrant and the properties that ground it." In contrast, the externalist "holds that warrant need not depend upon factors relevantly internal to the cognizer; warrant depends or supervenes upon properties of some of which the cognizer may have no special access, or even no epistemic access at all" (*Warrant*, 5–6).

6. In *Epistemology and Cognition* Goldman points out, "Theories that invoke solely psychological conditions of the cognizer are naturally called 'subjective,' or 'internalist,' theories. Theories that invoke such matters as the actual truth or falsity of relevant propositions are naturally called 'externalist' theories (assuming, at any rate, some realist approach to truth)" (24).

7. Nicholas Lash, in his introduction, rightly points out that one of the reasons that Newman's chapter on the illative sense in the *Grammar* (chapter 9) "is comparatively short is because it is to some extent recapitulatory, bringing into explicit focus matters that, before the introduction of the technical term 'illative sense,' have already been under discussion in the earlier chapters of Part Two" (*GA* 17). Thus, my references to the illative sense are not restricted to chapter 9 in the *Grammar*.

8. For example, Frank M. Turner assumes that Newman's dissatisfaction with the conceptions of rationality in his day implies a repudiation of reason and an endorsement of skepticism. *John Henry Newman: The Challenge to Evangelical Religion* (New Haven: Yale University Press, 2002). However, Turner misses the complexities and subtleties of Newman's epistemic proposal—a broader account of rationality than the options of fideism and evidentialism.

9. On this point, see Alston, *Beyond Justification*, 52–57; Roberts and Wood, *Intellectual Virtues*, 36–39. Moser makes a similar observation about "two different notions of a regulative reason at work in current debates over internalism and externalism about reasons for action. The resulting lesson is that internalists and

externalists about practical reasons are actually talking about different matters (at least at a level of specificity), not disagreeing about some particular matter." Thus, "one's aims in adopting and using notions of rationality, reasons, and obligations can cogently recommend, at least to oneself, an internalist or an externalist notion of rationality, reasons, and obligations" (*Philosophy after Objectivity*, 152). Swinburne concludes that "the many different internalist and externalist theories of justification are not rival theories of the same concept, but accounts of different concepts" (*Epistemic Justification*, 190–191). Given the different aims of each in mind, a fruitful study would involve determining the connections between externalist and internalist aspects of cognition and the process of rendering judgments.

10. My focus on proper fit resembles William Abraham's "principle of appropriate epistemic fit." Abraham argues that the fit between our theories of "rationality, justification, knowledge, warrant, and the like, should be appropriate to the subject matter in hand" (*Crossing the Threshold*, 11). However, my emphasis is more on the context- and agent-specific aspects of rendering apt judgments about the issues at hand.

11. Drawing on Alston's epistemic desiderata approach, Roberts and Wood make an observation comparable to what I have in mind in this chapter: "A natural way to bring together the diverse epistemic desiderata is in a *person* who has the power, inclination, and intelligent flexibility to meet the demands for these desiderata *as occasion arises*" (*Intellectual Virtues*, 36).

12. For further discussion about the "prior grounding requirement," see Williams, *Problems of Knowledge*. For example, Williams points out that "it is not obvious that all justification is like this [giving grounds for inferring further facts]. Many of our beliefs result from the unreflective use of our perceptual capacities and, in such cases, talk of evidence [or access to the grounds for a belief] seems strained. . . . In general, many beliefs are credible because they derive from a reliable source. Such sources could include the testimony of a dependable witness, a book written by an accredited authority, or direct personal observation under favourable conditions. So while justification may involve citing evidence for one's beliefs, it can also involve giving one's credentials or tracing one's belief to some reliable process of belief-formation" (25).

13. Newman says essentially the same in the following letters: "By instinct [spontaneous impulse . . . leading to a result without assignable or recognizable intellectual media (August 20, 1869)] I mean realization of a particular; by intuition, of a general fact—in both cases without assignable or recognizable media of realization. . . . But I consider Ratiocination far higher, more subtle, wider, and more certain than logical Inference—and its principle of action is the Illative Sense" (August 18, 1869; Ward 2:258). Again, Newman in talking about perception means: "I perceive by instinct (as I call it) without argumentative media" (August 21, 1869; Ward 2:259), to which Ward adds, "To the power of spontaneous action in human reason, whereby it draws its conclusions from premises of which it is only in part explicitly conscious, and judges those conclusions to be

warranted, he [Newman] gives the name of the 'illative sense'" (Ward 2:263).

14. See Hassin, Uleman, and Bargh, *The New Unconscious*.

15. Wilson, *Strangers to Ourselves*, 5. For a contemporary discussion of the two levels of human cognition, see Jonathan St. B. T. Evans and Keith Frankish, *In Two Minds: Dual Processes and Beyond* (Oxford: Oxford University Press, 2009).

16. Wilson, *Strangers to Ourselves*, 5, 23, 26.

17. Ibid., 43–44.

18. For example, "Implicit and Explicit Reason" (*US* XIII), "Wisdom, as Contrasted with Faith and with Bigotry" (*US* XIV), and the distinction between simple and complex assents (*GA*, esp. chapter 6).

19. Ferreira makes a similar point: "Newman's two roles of the will effectively distinguish between two kinds of commitment—a non-deliberative passive adherence and a deliberative active adherence." *Doubt and Religious Commitment*, 9.

20. Tilley, *Wisdom of Religious Commitment*, 135.

21. Robert Brandom sets forth a helpful distinction between the implicit and the explicit: "We might think of the process of expression in the more complex and interesting cases as a matter not of transforming what is inner into what is outer but of making *explicit* what is *implicit*. This can be understood in a pragmatist sense of turning something we can initially only *do* into something we *say*: codifying some sort of knowing *how* in the form of a knowing *that*." *Articulating Reasons: An Introduction to Inferentialism* (Cambridge, MA: Harvard University Press, 2001), 8.

22. As Williams points out, "*purely* or *radically*" externalist accounts contend that "external factors *alone* give sufficient conditions for knowledge." Likewise, "purely internalist" accounts "deny that external factors are ever relevant to a belief's epistemic status." Yet, there seems to be "no immediately obvious reason why an acceptable theory of knowledge should take either of these pure forms." *Problems of Knowledge*, 32.

23. The relation of the moral and the intellectual is a complex issue in Newman.

24. Brandom, *Articulating Reasons*, 61.

25. Robin C. Selby argues that Newman falls in line with the philosophical tradition (e.g., Locke) that claimed that philosophical reflection must be grounded in the philosophy of mind. *The Principle of Reserve in the Writings of John Henry Cardinal Newman* (Oxford: Oxford University Press, 1975), 16.

26. On this distinction, see Heather Battaly, "Virtue Epistemology," *Philosophy Compass* 3 (2008): 639–666; Roberts and Wood, *Intellectual Virtues*.

27. In a letter to William Froude on April 29, 1879, Newman wrote, "there is a faculty in the mind which I think I have called the inductive sense, which, when properly cultivated and used, answers to Aristotle's φρόνησις, its province being, not virtue, but the 'inquisitio veri,' which decides for us, beyond any technical rules, when, how, etc. to pass from inference to assent, and when and under what circumstances, etc. etc. not" (*L&D* 30:148).

28. For further discussion concerning the connection between Newman's and

Aristotle's notions of the illative sense, see Tillman, "Economies of Reason," 45–53; Gérard Verbeke, "Aristotelian Roots of Newman's Illative Sense," in *Newman and Gladstone Centennial Essays*, ed. James D. Bastable (Dublin: Veritas, 1978), 177–195.

29. Christopher Hookway, "Epistemology and Inquiry: The Primacy of Practice," in *Epistemology Futures*, ed. Stephen Hetherington (Oxford: Clarendon Press, 2006), 108.

30. Newman, *Theological Papers*, 127.

31. I recognize that this distinction in the *Grammar* is not always neat and clear, but it seems to stand at the end of the day. As Ferreira points out, however, for Newman, assents "or more precisely those propositions to which we assent are not for that reason indubitable. Some kind of dubitability is implied in the criticizability or corrigibility of these assents." *Doubt and Religious Commitment*, 91.

32. Sosa, *Knowledge in Perspective*, 145. See also Ernest Sosa, *A Virtue Epistemology: Apt Belief and Reflective Knowledge* (Oxford: Clarendon Press, 2007), vol. 1, especially lecture 2.

33. Kvanvig, *Value of Knowledge*, 206.

34. Sosa, *Knowledge in Perspective*, 240.

35. Ernest Sosa, *Reflective Knowledge: Apt Belief and Reflective Knowledge* (Oxford: Clarendon Press, 2009), 2:136–137.

36. Greco, "Virtues in Epistemology," in *The Oxford Handbook of Epistemology*, ed. Paul Moser (New York: Oxford University Press, 2002), 301. Kvanvig adds, "Sosa's description of reflective knowledge seems very much like the theory of understanding" (*Value of Knowledge*, 206).

37. John R. T. Lamont, "Newman on Faith and Rationality," *International Journal for Philosophy of Religion* 40 (1996): 81.

38. Dunne, *Back to the Rough Ground*, 368. In *Communities of Informed Judgment*, I unearth and develop a constructive link between Newman's account of judgment (and epistemic dependence) and recent work in social epistemology and virtue epistemology.

39. Wainwright, *Reason and the Heart*, 66.

40. Ferreira points out that "Newman sets forth what C. S. Peirce, Wittgenstein, and others would later maintain—namely, universal doubt is unreasonable since we need grounds for doubting" (*Doubt and Religious Commitment*, 95). See also William Alston, *The Reliability of Sense Perception* (Ithaca, NY: Cornell University Press, 1993).

41. On the explanatory aspect of understanding, see Kvanvig, *Value of Knowledge*, and Riggs, "Understanding 'Virtue.'"

42. The language of obligation resembles the Lockean notion of justification as an epistemic duty. See *An Essay Concerning Human Understanding*, especially Book 4. Perhaps Newman concedes that Locke's conception applies to people who are capable of engaging in such a task. Formally speaking, a person is "properly blamed for failing to do something *A* if and only if it is your duty to do *A* (and you fail to do it)" (Plantinga, *Warrant*, 15).

43. For a fascinating and concrete discussion of epistemic humility, see Robert C. Roberts and W. Jay Wood, "Humility and Epistemic Goods," in DePaul and Zagzebski, *Intellectual Virtue*, 257–279.

44. In *Communities of Informed Judgment*, I transpose the problem of the common measure (an independent standard of justification) in the *Grammar* into a problem of trusting the illative sense as a reliable belief-forming process.

45. On the relationship between externalism and epistemic responsibility, see Guy Axtell, "Blind Man's Bluff: The Basic Belief Apologetic as Anti-skeptical Stratagem," *Philosophical Studies* (2006): 131–152.

46. Stephen Hetherington, "How to Know (that Knowledge-that is Knowledge-how)," in *Epistemology Futures*, ed. Stephen Hetherington (Oxford: Clarendon Press, 2006), 78.

47. Brandom argues that "knowledge based on reliability without the subject's having reasons for it is possible as a local phenomenon, but not as a global one." Moreover, "it is at the very least unclear that we can make sense of a community of believers who, while often holding true beliefs, and generally acquiring them by reliable mechanisms, *never* are in a position to offer reasons for their beliefs. This would require that they never take themselves or one another to be reliable" (*Articulating Reasons*, 106–107).

48. Moser, *Philosophy after Objectivity*, 15.

49. Battaly, "Virtue Epistemology," 652.

50. In my estimation, Terrence Merrigan's notion of the union of clear heads and holy hearts makes a similar move; see his *Clear Heads and Holy Hearts*. Nagel, in *The View from Nowhere*, provides a fascinating discussion of the dialectical relationship between the subjective and objective dimensions of knowledge.

51. See Linda T. Zagzebski, "Recovering Understanding," in *Knowledge, Truth, and Duty: Essays on Epistemic Justification, Responsibility, and Virtue*, ed. Matthias Steup (Oxford: Oxford University Press, 2001), 235–251; Riggs, "Understanding 'Virtue'"; Wayne Riggs, "Reliability and the Value of Knowledge," *Philosophy and Phenomenological Research* 64 (2002): 79–96; Elgin, *Considered Judgment*; Kvanvig, *Value of Knowledge*.

52. Linda T. Zagzebski, *Virtues of the Mind: An Inquiry into the Nature of Virtue and the Ethical Foundations of Knowledge* (Cambridge: Cambridge University Press, 1996), 21.

53. Riggs, "Understanding 'Virtue'," 218, 213.

54. Selby, *The Principle of Reserve*, 101.

55. On the distinction between reflective and unreflective aspects of understanding, see Roberts and Wood, *Intellectual Virtues*, 48–49.

56. On this point, see Pollock, "Irrationality and Cognition"; Gigerenzer, Todd, and the ABC Research Group, *Simple Heuristics*; Wilson, *Strangers to Ourselves*; Fauconnier and Turner, *The Way We Think*; Hassin, Uleman, and Bargh, *The New Unconscious*.

57. Williams, *Problems of Knowledge*, 34.

58. For further reflection, see Roberts and Wood, *Intellectual Virtues*.

3—A CONNECTED VIEW

1. Martha Nussbaum, *Cultivating Humanity: A Classical Defense of Reform in Liberal Education* (Cambridge, MA: Harvard University Press, 1997), makes a similar point in her argument for the educational formation of citizens of the world. See also Nussbaum, *Not for Profit: Why Democracy Needs the Humanities* (Princeton, NJ: Princeton University Press, 2010).

2. David Ford rightly raises and tackles the question of "whether there is a strong case for a world class university to be committed to keeping" teaching and research together. *Christian Wisdom: Desiring God and Learning in Love* (Cambridge: Cambridge University Press, 2007), 317. However, I do not take up this question. I simply acknowledge the difference between Newman's context and ours on the scope and aims of university education.

3. Ford makes a similar observation: "The dimension of formation through university education is one of the least discussed at present." For Ford, the overall picture of intellectual formation "is of learning patterns that form intellectual virtues, values and skills which can shape a lifetime of further learning, and that involve informal, sociable cross-disciplinary engagement, shaping a horizon in which other disciplines make sense" (*Christian Wisdom*, 320, 321). Louis Menand concludes that the "key to reform of almost any kind in higher education lies not in the way that knowledge is produced. It lies in the way that the producers of knowledge are produced." *The Marketplace of Ideas: Reform and Resistance in the American University* (New York: W. W. Norton, 2010), 157.

4. Noel Annan rightly points out that, for Newman, the university was primarily a place for teaching universal knowledge. Thus, it "did not exist to *create* knowledge. Its purpose was to disseminate 'the best that is known and thought in the world', to use Matthew Arnold's words. Of course, the teachers should 'study', but the notion of systematic research did not swim into Newman's ken. Originality, discovery, students dedicated to a single branch of learning, were contrary to his idea of a university." Noel Annan, *The Dons: Mentors, Eccentrics, and Geniuses* (Chicago: University of Chicago Press, 1999), 53.

5. Randall Collins argues, "although lectures, discussions, conferences, and other real-time gatherings would be superfluous in a world of texts, it is exactly these face-to-face structures which are most constant across the entire history of intellectual life." *The Sociology of Philosophies: A Global Theory of Intellectual Change* (Cambridge: Harvard University Press, 1998), 25.

6. For example, recent work in virtue epistemology, value-driven epistemology, naturalized epistemology, and social epistemology requires an interdisciplinary scope of mind.

7. John Holloway, *The Victorian Sage* (New York: Norton, 1965), 9. Michael P. Lynch says that a fundamental task of philosophy, following Wittgenstein, is to "assemble reminders," that is, to "point out to us what has been right there in front of our face all along. While this isn't all that a philosopher does, there is a lot of sense in this point. The very familiarity of something can make us forget, or even deny its importance. When that happens, we need to be reminded of its role in our everyday life." *True to Life: Why Truth Matters* (Cambridge, MA: MIT Press, 2004), 10. This aspect of philosophy squares with the notion of an integrative habit of mind.

8. Newman preached this sermon on Whit-Tuesday, 1841. Ian Ker points out that this sermon contains "respectively the genesis of *The Idea of a University.*" *John Henry Newman: A Biography* (Oxford: Oxford University Press, 1988), 264.

9. John Kekes, *Pluralism in Philosophy: Changing the Subject* (Ithaca, NY: Cornell University Press, 2000), 7.

10. Thomas Nagel, *The Last Word* (New York: Oxford University Press, 1997), 129, 130.

11. Ibid., 130, 131.

12. Confirmed in an email correspondence with Professor Nagel (March 3, 2009).

13. Nagel, *The Last Word*, 132, 131.

14. Nagel, *The View from Nowhere*, 15; Nagel, *The Last Word*, 131.

15. See also discourses 4 and 5 in the *Idea*.

16. Elgin describes such activity as reflective equilibrium: "And a measure of the adequacy of a new finding is its fit with what we think we already understand. If the finding is at all surprising, the background of accepted beliefs is apt to require modification to make room for it; and the finding may require revision to fit into place. . . . A process of delicate adjustments takes place, its goal being a system in wide reflective equilibrium. Coherence alone will not suffice. A system is coherent if its components mesh. Reflective equilibrium requires more. The components of a system in reflective equilibrium must be reasonable in light of one another, and the system as a whole must be reasonable in light of our antecedent commitments about the subject at hand" (*Considered Judgment*, 13).

17. Joshua Hochschild, "The Re-imagined Aristotelianism of John Henry Newman," *Modern Age* 45 (2003): 336. On this point, see also Jaroslav Pelikan, *The Idea of the University: A Reexamination* (New Haven: Yale University Press, 1992), 35.

18. Kvanvig, *Value of Knowledge*, 192.

19. John Henry Newman, *Rise and Progress of Universities and Benedictine Essays* (Notre Dame, IN: University of Notre Dame Press, 2001), henceforth cited as *Rise*, XXXVII, XXXIX. Svaglic points out that "Newman was most powerfully drawn to and influenced by those in whom the intellectual complemented the moral and religious life—a Keble, a Froude, or a Pusey at Oxford, Clement, Origen, Augustine, and the great church of Alexandria among the Fathers. . . . [This

is what we might call] the *ethos* of the place: above all by the influence of teachers who themselves exemplified, however, imperfectly, the Christian humanist ideal" (*Idea* XXIII).

20. Nancy Sherman, *The Fabric of Character: Aristotle's Theory of Virtue* (Oxford: Clarendon Press, 1989), 30. Isaiah Berlin captures well the importance of professorial guidance in helping students to see or make connections: "If this task is to be performed, it can be accomplished not by precept but only by example—by the discovery or training of teachers of sufficient knowledge, imagination, and talent to make the students see what they see: an experience which, as anyone knows who has ever had a good teacher of any subject, is always fascinating, and can be transforming." *The Power of Ideas*, ed. Henry Hardy (Princeton, NJ: Princeton University Press, 2001), 219.

21. On this point, for example, see DePaul and Zagzebski, *Intellectual Virtue*.

22. Edward Craig, *Knowledge and the State of Nature* (Oxford: Clarendon Press, 1990), 36.

23. Ford, *Christian Wisdom*, 324.

24. James M. Banner, Jr., and Harold C. Cannon, *The Elements of Teaching* (New Haven: Yale University Press, 1997), 4.

25. Ford, *Christian Wisdom*, 318.

26. Michael J. Buckley, *The Catholic University as Promise and Project* (Washington, DC: Georgetown University Press, 1998), 170.

27. Parker J. Palmer, *The Courage to Teach: Exploring the Inner Landscape of a Teacher's Life* (San Francisco: Jossey-Bass, 1998), 127.

28. Peter C. Hodgson, *God's Wisdom: Toward a Theology of Education* (Louisville, KY: Westminster/John Knox Press, 1999), 62.

29. Palmer, *Courage to Teach*, 104.

30. Ibid., 11.

31. On this point, see Jerome Bruner, *The Culture of Education* (Cambridge, MA: Harvard University Press, 1996). See also Christine Korsgaard, *Self-constitution: Agency, Identity, and Integrity* (Oxford: Oxford University Press, 2009).

32. Nussbaum, *Cultivating Humanity*, 14, 62.

33. Banner and Cannon, *Elements of Teaching*, 16.

34. Howard Gardner, *Intelligence Reframed: Multiple Intelligences for the 21st Century* (New York: Basic Books, 1999), 152. For further discussion of learning styles and multiple intelligences, see Robert J. Sternberg, *Thinking Styles* (Cambridge: Cambridge University Press, 1997); Kieran Egan, *The Educated Mind: How Cognitive Tools Shape Our Understanding* (Chicago and London: University of Chicago Press, 1997); Howard Gardner, *Frames of Mind: The Theory of Multiple Intelligences*, 2nd ed. (New York: Basic Books, 1993).

35. Banner and Cannon, *Elements of Teaching*, 3.

36. On this point, Newman quotes from Aristotle's *Nicomachean Ethics*: "A well-educated man will expect exactness in every class of subject, according as the nature of things admits; for it is much the same mistake to put up with a

mathematician using probabilities, and to require demonstration of an orator. Each man judges skillfully in those things about which he is well-informed; it is of these that he is a good judge; viz. he, in each subject-matter is a judge, who is well-educated in that subject-matter, and he is in an absolute sense a judge, who is in all of them well-educated. . . . Young men come to be mathematicians and the like, but they cannot possess practical judgment; for this talent is employed upon individual facts, and these are learned only by experience; and a youth has not experience, for experience is only gained by a course of years. And so, again, it would appear that a boy may be a mathematician, but not a philosopher, or learned in physics, and for this reason,—because the one study deals with abstractions, while the other studies gain their principles from experience, and in the latter subjects youths do not give assent, but make assertions, but in the former they know what it is that they are handling" (*GA* 322).

37. John Henry Newman, *The Philosophical Notebook of John Henry Newman*, ed. Edward Sillem, 2 vols. (Louvain: Nauwelaerts, 1969–1970), 1:87–88. For further reflection on the communal nature of epistemic reflection in Newman's notion of the illative sense, see Aquino, *Communities of Informed Judgment*.

38. Vincent F. Blehl, "The Role of Education in the Formation of Conscience and the Illative Sense," *Newman Studien* 11 (1980): 145.

39. Newman, *Theological Papers*, 27. For some recent discussion about the nature, scope, and function of testimony and the role of epistemic dependence and expertise in epistemology, see Jennifer Lackey and Ernest Sosa, ed., *The Epistemology of Testimony* (Oxford: Oxford University Press, 2006); Robert Crease and Evan Selinger, eds., *The Philosophy of Expertise* (New York: Columbia University Press, 2006). For a fascinating and illuminating account of the connection between justice and testimony, see Miranda Fricker, *Epistemic Injustice* (Oxford: Oxford University Press, 2008).

40. For further reflection, see Frederick D. Aquino, "The Craft of Teaching: The Relevance of Newman for Theological Education," *Christian Higher Education* 2 (2003): 269–284.

41. Nagel, *View from Nowhere*, 6.

42. Riggs, "Understanding 'Virtue,'" 214. Newman seems to agree that success is not a necessary condition of being intellectually virtuous.

43. Martha Nussbaum, *The Therapy of Desire: Theory and Practice in Hellenistic Ethics* (Princeton, NJ: Princeton University Press, 1994), 337.

44. Ibid., 345.

45. See Hadot, *Philosophy as a Way of Life*.

46. For a fascinating discussion about the interdisciplinary dimensions of human selfhood, see Dan Zahavi, *Subjectivity and Selfhood: Investigating the First-Person Perspective* (Cambridge, MA: MIT Press, 2005).

47. Paul Thagard, *Mind: Introduction to Cognitive Science*, 2nd ed. (Cambridge, MA: MIT Press, 2005), 7.

48. Bruner, *Culture of Education*, 20.

49. Ford, *Christian Wisdom*, 335.

AFTERWORD

1. Robert Nozick, *The Examined Life: Philosophical Meditations* (New York: Simon and Schuster, 1989), 15.

2. On this point, see Abraham, *Canon and Criterion.*

3. Tilley, *Wisdom of Religious Commitment*, 156–157.

4. On the connection between testimonial injustices and epistemology, see Fricker, *Epistemic Injustice*; Bernard Williams, *Truth and Truthfulness: An Essay in Genealogy* (Princeton, NJ: Princeton University Press).

5. Fricker, *Epistemic Injustice*, 120.

6. On this point, see Moser, *Philosophy after Objectivity*, especially chapter 4.

References

Abraham, William J. *Canon and Criterion in Christian Theology: From the Fathers to Feminism*. Oxford: Clarendon Press, 1998.

——. *Crossing the Threshold of Divine Revelation*. Grand Rapids, MI: Eerdmans, 2006.

Abraham, William J., Jason E. Vickers, and Natalie Van Kirk, eds. *Canonical Theism: A Proposal for Theology and the Church*. Grand Rapids, MI: Eerdmans, 2008.

Alston, William P. *Epistemic Justification: Essays in the Theory of Knowledge*. Ithaca, NY: Cornell University Press, 1989.

——. *Perceiving God: The Epistemology of Religious Experience*. Ithaca, NY: Cornell University Press, 1991.

——. "Epistemic Desiderata." *Philosophy and Phenomenological Research* 53 (1993): 527–551.

——. *The Reliability of Sense Perception*. Ithaca, NY: Cornell University Press, 1993.

——. *Beyond Justification: Dimensions of Epistemic Evaluation*. Ithaca, NY: Cornell University Press, 2005.

Annan, Noel. *The Dons: Mentors, Eccentrics, and Geniuses*. Chicago: University of Chicago Press, 1999.

Annas, Julia. *The Morality of Happiness*. New York: Oxford University Press, 1993.

Aquino, Frederick D. "The Craft of Teaching: The Relevance of Newman for Theological Education." *Christian Higher Education* 2 (2003): 269–284.

——. *Communities of Informed Judgment: Newman and Accounts of Rationality*. Washington, DC: Catholic University of America Press, 2004.

——. "Broadening Horizons: Constructing an Epistemology of Religious Belief." *Louvain Studies* 30.3 (2005): 198–213.

——. "Externalism and Internalism: A Newmanian Matter of Proper Fit." *Heythrop Journal* 51 (2010): 1023–1034.

——. "Thick and Thin: Personal and Communal Dimensions of Communicating Faith." In *Communicating Faith*, ed. John Sullivan, 199–213. Washington, DC: Catholic University of America Press, 2010.

Aristotle. *Nicomachean Ethics*. Translated by Terrence Irwin. 2nd ed. Indianapolis, IN: Hackett, 1999.

Audi, Robert. *The Structure of Justification*. Cambridge: Cambridge University Press, 1993.

——. *Religious Commitment and Secular Reason*. Cambridge: Cambridge University Press, 2000.

Axtell, Guy. "Blind Man's Bluff: The Basic Belief Apologetic as Anti-Skeptical Stratagem." *Philosophical Studies* (2006): 131–152.

Axtell, Guy, and J. Adam Carter. "Just the Right Thickness: A Defense of Second-Wave Virtue Epistemology." *Philosophical Papers* 37 (2008): 413–434.

116   *References*

Banner, James M., Jr., and Harold C. Cannon. *The Elements of Teaching.* New Haven: Yale University Press, 1997.

Barnes, Eric Christian. *The Paradox of Predictivism.* Cambridge: Cambridge University Press, 2008.

Battaly, Heather. "Virtue Epistemology." *Philosophy Compass* 3 (2008): 639–666.

Bergmann, Michael. *Justification without Awareness: A Defense of Epistemic Externalism.* Oxford: Clarendon Press, 2006.

Berlin, Isaiah. *The Power of Ideas.* Edited by Henry Hardy. Princeton, NJ: Princeton University Press, 2001.

Blehl, Vincent F. "The Role of Education in the Formation of Conscience and the Illative Sense." *Newman Studien* 11 (1980): 143–149.

Boekraad, A. J. *Personal Quest of Truth.* Louvain: Nauwelaerts, 1955.

———. *The Argument from Conscience to the Existence of God according to J. H. Newman.* Louvain: Nauwelaerts, 1961.

Brandom, Robert. *Articulating Reasons: An Introduction to Inferentialism.* Cambridge, MA: Harvard University Press, 2001.

Bruner, Jerome. *The Culture of Education.* Cambridge, MA: Harvard University Press, 1996.

Buckley, Michael J. *The Catholic University as Promise and Project.* Washington, DC: Georgetown University Press, 1998.

Cameron, J. M. *The Night Battle.* London: Burns and Oates, 1962.

Carr, Thomas K. *Newman and Gadamer: Toward a Hermeneutics of Religious Knowledge.* Atlanta, GA: Scholars Press, 1996.

Cavell, Stanley. *Cities of Words: Pedagogical Letters on a Register of the Moral Life.* Cambridge, MA: The Belknap Press of Harvard University Press, 2004.

Charry, Ellen T. *By the Renewing of Your Minds: The Pastoral Function of Christian Doctrine.* Oxford: Oxford University Press, 1997.

Chisholm, Roderick M. *The Problem of the Criterion.* Milwaukee: Marquette University Press, 1973.

Coakley, Sarah. *Powers and Submissions: Spirituality, Gender, and Philosophy.* Oxford: Blackwell, 2002.

Collingwood, Robin G. *Speculum Mentis or The Map of Knowledge.* Oxford: Clarendon Press, 1956.

Collins, Randall. *The Sociology of Philosophies: A Global Theory of Intellectual Change.* Cambridge, MA: Harvard University Press, 1998.

Connolly, William. *Capitalism and Christianity, American Style.* Durham, NC: Duke University Press, 2008.

Cottingham, John. *The Spiritual Dimension: Religion, Philosophy and Value.* Cambridge: Cambridge University Press, 2005.

Coulson, John. "Newman's Hour: The Significance of Newman's Thought, and Its Application Today." *Heythrop Journal* 22 (1981): 394–406.

Craig, Edward. *Knowledge and the State of Nature.* Oxford: Clarendon Press, 1990.

Crease, Robert, and Evan Selinger, eds. *The Philosophy of Expertise.* New York: Columbia University Press, 2006.

DePaul, Michael, and Linda Zagzebski, eds. *Intellectual Virtue: Perspectives from Ethics and Epistemology.* Oxford: Clarendon Press, 2003.

Dretske, Fred. *Knowledge and the Flow of Information.* Cambridge, MA: MIT Press, 1981.

Dunne, Joseph. *Back to the Rough Ground: Practical Judgment and the Lure of Technique.* Notre Dame, IN: University of Notre Dame Press, 1992.

Eberle, Christopher. *Religious Conviction in Liberal Politics.* Cambridge: Cambridge University Press, 2002.

Egan, Kieran. *The Educated Mind: How Cognitive Tools Shape Our Understanding.* Chicago: University of Chicago Press, 1997.

Elgin, Catherine Z. *Considered Judgment.* Princeton, NJ: Princeton University Press, 1996.

Evans, Jonathan St. B. T., and Keith Frankish. *In Two Minds: Dual Processes and Beyond.* Oxford: Oxford University Press, 2009.

Fauconnier, Gilles, and Mark Turner. *The Way We Think: Conceptual Blending and the Mind's Hidden Complexities.* New York: Basic Books, 2002.

Ferreira, M. Jamie. *Doubt and Religious Commitment: The Role of the Will in Newman's Thought.* Oxford: Clarendon Press, 1980.

———. *Scepticism and Reasonable Doubt: The British Naturalist Tradition in Wilkins, Hume, Reid and Newman.* Oxford: Clarendon Press, 1986.

Fey, William R. *Faith and Doubt: The Unfolding of Newman's Thought on Certainty.* Shepherdstown, WV: Patmos Press, 1976.

Foley, Richard. "Egoism in Epistemology." In *Socializing Epistemology: The Social Dimensions of Knowledge,* ed. Frederick F. Schmitt, 53–73. Lanham, MD: Rowman and Littlefield, 1994.

———. "Conceptual Diversity in Epistemology." In *Contemporary Debates in Epistemology,* ed. Matthias Steup and Ernest Sosa, 177–203. Oxford: Blackwell, 2005.

Ford, David. *Christian Wisdom: Desiring God and Learning in Love.* Cambridge: Cambridge University Press, 2007.

Ford, John T. "Recent Studies on Newman: Two Review Articles." *The Thomist* 41 (1977): 424–440.

Fricker, Miranda. *Epistemic Injustice.* Oxford: Oxford University Press, 2008.

Gardner, Howard. *Frames of Mind: The Theory of Multiple Intelligences.* 2nd ed. New York: Basic Books, 1993.

———. *Intelligence Reframed: Multiple Intelligences for the 21st Century.* New York: Basic Books, 1999.

Gendler, Tamar Szabó, and John Hawthorne, eds. *Oxford Studies in Epistemology.* Vol. 3. Oxford: Oxford University Press, 2010.

Gigerenzer, Gerd, Peter M. Todd, and the ABC Research Group. *Simple Heuristics That Make Us Smart.* New York: Oxford University Press, 1999.

Glover, Jonathan. *Humanity: A Moral History of the Twentieth Century.* New Haven: Yale University Press, 1999.

Goldberg, Sanford. *Anti-individualism: Mind and Language, Knowledge and Justification.* Cambridge: Cambridge University Press, 2007.

———. *Relying on Others: An Essay in Epistemology.* Oxford: Oxford University Press, 2010.

Goldie, Peter. "Seeing What Is the Kind Thing to Do: Perception and Emotion in Morality." *Dialectica* 61 (2007): 347–361.

Goldman, Alvin I. *Epistemology and Cognition.* Cambridge, MA: Harvard University Press, 1986.

———. *Knowledge in a Social World.* Oxford: Clarendon Press, 1999.

———. *Pathways to Knowledge: Private and Public.* Oxford: Oxford University Press, 2002.

Greco, John. *Putting Skeptics in Their Place: The Nature of Skeptical Arguments and Their Role in Philosophical Inquiry.* Cambridge: Cambridge University Press, 2000.

———. "Virtues and Rules in Epistemology." In *Virtue Epistemology: Essays on Epistemic Virtue and Responsibility*, ed. Abrol Fairweather and Linda Zagzebski, 117–141. Oxford: Oxford University Press, 2001.

———. "Virtues in Epistemology." In *The Oxford Handbook of Epistemology*, ed. Paul Moser, 287–315. New York: Oxford University Press, 2002.

———. *Achieving Knowledge: A Virtue-Theoretic Account of Epistemic Normativity.* Cambridge: Cambridge University Press, 2010.

———. "Seeing Good, Seeing God: The Epistemology of Moral and Religious Experience." Unpublished paper, 1–14.

Greenawalt, Kent. *Religious Conviction and Political Choice.* Oxford: Oxford University Press, 1988.

Haddon, Mark. *The Curious Incident of the Dog in the Night-Time.* New York: Vantage, 2003.

Hadot, Pierre. *Philosophy as a Way of Life: Spiritual Exercises from Socrates to Foucault.* Oxford: Blackwell, 1995.

———. *What Is Ancient Philosophy?* Translated by Michael Chase. Cambridge, MA: The Belknap Press of Harvard University Press, 2002.

Harper, Gordon H., ed. *Cardinal Newman and William Froude, FRS: A Correspondence.* Baltimore: Johns Hopkins Press, 1933.

Harris, Harriet A. "Does Analytical Philosophy Clip Our Wings? Reformed Epistemology as a Test Case." In *Faith and Philosophical Analysis: The Impact of Analytical Philosophy of Religion on the Philosophy of Religion*, ed. Harriet A. Harris and Christopher J. Insole, 100–118. Aldershot: Ashgate, 2005.

Hassin, Ran R., James S. Uleman, and John A. Bargh, eds. *The New Unconscious.* New York: Oxford University Press, 2005.

Hetherington, Stephen. "How to Know (that Knowledge-that is Knowledge-how)." In *Epistemology Futures*, ed. Stephen Hetherington, 71–94. Oxford: Clarendon Press, 2006.

Hochschild, Joshua. "The Re-imagined Aristotelianism of John Henry Newman." *Modern Age* 45 (2003): 333–342.

Hodgson, Peter C. *God's Wisdom: Toward a Theology of Education.* Louisville, KY: Westminster/John Knox Press, 1999.

Holloway, John. *The Victorian Sage*. New York: Norton, 1965.

Hookway, Christopher. "Epistemology and Inquiry: The Primacy of Practice." In *Epistemology Futures*, ed. Stephen Hetherington, 95–110. Oxford: Clarendon Press, 2006.

Huemer, Michael. *Skepticism and the Veil of Perception*. Lanham, MD: Rowman and Littlefield, 2001.

Kekes, John. *Pluralism in Philosophy: Changing the Subject*. Ithaca, NY: Cornell University Press, 2000.

Ker, Ian T. *John Henry Newman: A Biography*. Oxford: Oxford University Press, 1988.

King, Benjamin J. *Newman and the Alexandrian Fathers: Shaping Doctrine in Nineteenth-Century England*. Oxford: Clarendon Press, 2009.

Korsgaard, Christine. *Self-constitution: Agency, Identity, and Integrity*. Oxford: Oxford University Press, 2009.

Kvanvig, Jonathan. *The Intellectual Virtues and the Life of the Mind*. Lanham, MD: Rowman and Littlefield, 1992.

———. *The Value of Knowledge and the Pursuit of Understanding*. New York: Cambridge University Press, 2003.

———. "Truth Is Not the Primary Epistemic Goal." In *Contemporary Debates in Epistemology*, ed. Matthias Steup and Ernest Sosa, 285–295. Oxford: Blackwell, 2005.

Lackey, Jennifer, and Ernest Sosa, eds. *The Epistemology of Testimony*. Oxford: Oxford University Press, 2006.

Lamont, John R. T. "Newman on Faith and Rationality." *International Journal for Philosophy of Religion* 40 (1996): 63–84.

Lash, Nicholas. *The Beginning and the End of Religion*. Cambridge: Cambridge University Press, 1996.

Lilla, Mark. *The Stillborn God: Religion, Politics, and the Modern West*. New York: Vintage, 2007.

Locke, John. *An Essay Concerning Human Understanding*. Edited by Peter H. Nidditch. Oxford: Clarendon Press, 1975.

———. *Some Thoughts Concerning Education; and Of the Conducts of the Understanding*. Edited by Ruth W. Grant and Nathan Tarcov. Indianapolis, IN: Hackett, 1996.

Louth, Andrew. *Discerning the Mystery: An Essay on the Nature of Theology*. Oxford: Clarendon Press, 1990.

Lynch, Michael P. *True to Life: Why Truth Matters*. Cambridge, MA: MIT Press, 2004.

Magill, Gerard. "Newman's Personal Reasoning: The Inspiration of the Early Church." *Irish Theological Quarterly* 58 (1992): 304–313.

———, ed. *Discourse and Context: An Interdisciplinary Study of John Henry Newman*. Carbondale: Southern Illinois University Press, 1993.

Mathewes, Charles. *A Theology of Public Life*. Cambridge: Cambridge University Press, 2008.

McDowell, John. *The Engaged Intellect: Philosophical Essays*. Cambridge, MA: Harvard University Press, 2009.

McIntosh, Mark. *Mystical Theology: The Integrity of Spirituality and Theology*. Oxford: Blackwell, 1998.

Menand, Louis. *The Marketplace of Ideas: Reform and Resistance in the American University*. New York: W. W. Norton, 2010.

Merrigan, Terrence. "Newman's Oriel Experience: Its Significance for His Life and Thought." *Bijdragen* 47 (1986): 192–211.

———. *Clear Heads and Holy Hearts: The Religious and Theological Ideal of John Henry Newman*. Louvain: Peeters Press, 1991.

———. "Christianity and the Non-Christian Religions in the Light of the Theology of John Henry Newman." *Irish Theological Quarterly* 68 (2003): 343–355.

———. "Newman and Theological Liberalism." *Theological Studies* 66 (2005): 605–621.

Mitchell, Basil. *The Justification of Religious Belief*. New York: Seabury Press, 1973.

———. "Newman as a Philosopher." In *Newman after a Hundred Years*, ed. Ian T. Ker and Alan G. Hill, 223–246. Oxford: Clarendon Press, 1990.

———. *Faith and Criticism*. Oxford: Clarendon Press, 1994.

Moleski, Martin X. *Personal Catholicism: The Theological Epistemologies of John Henry Newman and Michael Polanyi*. Washington, DC: Catholic University of America Press, 2000.

Moser, Paul K. *Philosophy after Objectivity: Making Sense in Perspective*. Oxford: Oxford University Press, 1993.

———. *The Elusive God: Reorienting Religious Epistemology*. Cambridge: Cambridge University Press, 2008.

Nagel, Thomas. *The View from Nowhere*. Oxford: Oxford University Press, 1989.

———. *Equality and Impartiality*. New York: Oxford University Press, 1991.

———. *The Last Word*. New York: Oxford University Press, 1997.

Nédoncelle, Maurice. *La Philosophie religieuse de John Henry Newman*. Strasburg, 1946.

Newman, John Henry. *Autobiographical Writings*. Edited by Henry Tristam. New York: Sheed and Ward, 1957.

———. *Apologia pro Vita Sua*. Edited by David DeLaura. New York: W. W. Norton, 1968.

———. *The Philosophical Notebook of John Henry Newman*. Edited by Edward Sillem. 2 vols. Louvain: Nauwelaerts, 1969–1970.

———. *Letters and Diaries of John Henry Newman*. Edited by Charles S. Dessain et al. Vols. 29–30. Oxford: Clarendon Press, 1976.

———. *Letters and Diaries of John Henry Newman*. Edited by Charles S. Dessain et al. Vol. 25. Oxford: Clarendon Press, 1973.

———. *The Theological Papers of John Henry Newman on Faith and Certainty*. Edited by Hugo M. de Achaval and J. Derek Holmes. Oxford: Clarendon Press, 1976.

——. *An Essay in Aid of a Grammar of Assent*. Introduction by Nicholas Lash. Notre Dame, IN: University of Notre Dame Press, 1979.

——. *The Idea of a University*. Edited by Martin J. Svaglic. Notre Dame, IN: University of Notre Dame Press, 1982.

——. *Fifteen Sermons Preached before the University of Oxford*. 3rd ed. Introduction by Mary Katherine Tillman. Notre Dame, IN: University of Notre Dame Press, 1996.

——. *Rise and Progress of Universities and Benedictine Essays*. Notre Dame, IN: University of Notre Dame Press, 2001.

Nozick, Robert. *The Examined Life: Philosophical Meditations*. New York: Simon and Schuster, 1989.

Nussbaum, Martha. *Love's Knowledge: Essays on Philosophy and Literature*. New York: Oxford University Press, 1990.

——. *The Therapy of Desire: Theory and Practice in Hellenistic Ethics*. Princeton, NJ: Princeton University Press, 1994.

——. *Cultivating Humanity: A Classical Defense of Reform in Liberal Education*. Cambridge, MA: Harvard University Press, 1997.

——. *Liberty of Conscience: In Defense of America's Tradition of Religious Equality*. New York: Basic Books, 2008.

——. *Not for Profit: Why Democracy Needs the Humanities*. Princeton, NJ: Princeton University Press, 2010.

Pailin, David A. *The Way to Faith: An Examination of Newman's Grammar of Assent as a Response to the Search for Certainty in Faith*. London: Epworth Press, 1969.

Palmer, G. E. H., Philip Sherrard, and Kallistos Ware, eds. *The Philokalia*. Vol. 2. London: Faber and Faber, 1981.

Palmer, Parker J. *The Courage to Teach: Exploring the Inner Landscape of a Teacher's Life*. San Francisco: Jossey-Bass, 1998.

Pelikan, Jaroslav. *The Idea of the University: A Reexamination*. New Haven: Yale University Press, 1992.

Plantinga, Alvin. *Warrant: The Current Debate*. New York: Oxford University Press, 1993.

Pollock, John L. "Irrationality and Cognition." In *Epistemology: New Essays*, ed. Quentin Smith, 249–275. Oxford: Oxford University Press, 2008.

Pritchard, Duncan. "Recent Work on Epistemic Value." *American Philosophical Quarterly* 44 (2007): 85–110.

Raz, Joseph. *Engaging Reason: On the Theory of Value and Action*. Oxford: Oxford University Press, 1999.

——. *Value, Respect, and Attachment*. Cambridge: Cambridge University Press, 2001.

Riggs, Wayne. "Reliability and the Value of Knowledge." *Philosophy and Phenomenological Research* 64 (2002): 79–96.

——. "Understanding 'Virtue' and the Virtue of Understanding." In *Intellectual Virtue: Perspectives from Ethics and Epistemology*, ed. Michael DePaul and Linda Zagzebski, 203–226. Oxford: Clarendon Press, 2003.

———. "The Value Turn in Epistemology." In *New Waves in Epistemology*, ed. Vincent F. Hendricks and Duncan Pritchard, 300–323. New York: Palgrave Macmillan, 2008.

Roberts, Robert C., and W. Jay Wood. "Humility and Epistemic Goods." In *Intellectual Virtue: Perspectives from Ethics and Epistemology*, ed. Michael DePaul and Linda Zagzebski, 257–279. Oxford: Clarendon Press, 2003.

———. *Intellectual Virtues: An Essay in Regulative Epistemology*. Oxford: Clarendon Press, 2007.

Schmitt, Frederick F., ed. *Socializing Epistemology: The Social Dimensions of Knowledge*. Lanham, MD: Rowman and Littlefield, 1994.

———. "Social Epistemology." In *The Blackwell Guide to Epistemology*, ed. John Greco and Ernest Sosa, 354–382. Oxford: Blackwell Publishers, 1999.

Selby, Robin C. *The Principle of Reserve in the Writings of John Henry Cardinal Newman*. Oxford: Oxford University Press, 1975.

Sherman, Nancy. *The Fabric of Character: Aristotle's Theory of Virtue*. Oxford: Clarendon Press, 1989.

Solomon, Robert. *The Joy of Philosophy: Thinking Thin versus the Passionate Life*. New York: Oxford University Press, 1999.

Sosa, Ernest. *Knowledge in Perspective: Selected Essays in Epistemology*. Cambridge: Cambridge University Press, 1991.

———. *A Virtue Epistemology: Apt Belief and Reflective Knowledge*. Vol. 1. Oxford: Clarendon Press, 2007.

———. *Reflective Knowledge: Apt Belief and Reflective Knowledge*. Vol. 2. Oxford: Clarendon Press, 2009.

Sternberg, Robert J. *Thinking Styles*. Cambridge: Cambridge University Press, 1997.

Stout, Jeffrey. *The Flight from Authority: Religion, Morality, and the Quest for Autonomy*. Notre Dame, IN: University of Notre Dame Press, 1981.

———. *Democracy and Tradition*. Princeton, NJ: Princeton University Press, 2004.

Swinburne, Richard. *Epistemic Justification*. Oxford: Clarendon Press, 2001.

Taylor, Charles. *Sources of the Self: The Making of the Modern Identity*. Cambridge, MA: Harvard University Press, 1989.

Thagard, Paul. *Mind: Introduction to Cognitive Science*. 2nd ed. Cambridge, MA: MIT Press, 2005.

Tiberius, Valerie. *The Reflective Life: Living Wisely with Our Limits*. New York: Oxford University Press, 2008.

Tilley, Terrence W. *The Wisdom of Religious Commitment*. Washington, DC: Georgetown University Press, 1995.

Tillman, Mary Katherine. "Economies of Reason: Newman and the Phronesis Tradition." In *Discourse and Context: An Interdisciplinary Study of John Henry Newman*, ed. Gerard Magill, 45–53. Carbondale: Southern Illinois University Press, 1993.

Tracy, David. *The Analogical Imagination: Christian Theology and the Culture of Pluralism*. New York: Crossroad, 1981.

Turner, Frank M. *John Henry Newman: The Challenge to Evangelical Religion.* New Haven: Yale University Press, 2002.

Vargish, Thomas. *Newman: The Contemplation of Mind.* Oxford: Clarendon Press, 1970.

Verbeke, Gérard. "Aristotelian Roots of Newman's Illative Sense." In *Newman and Gladstone Centennial Essays,* ed. James D. Bastable, 177–195. Dublin: Veritas, 1978.

Wainwright, William J. *Reason and the Heart: A Prolegomenon to a Critique of Passional Reason.* Ithaca, NY: Cornell University Press, 1995.

Walzer, Michael. *Thick and Thin: Moral Argument at Home and Abroad.* Notre Dame, IN: University of Notre Dame Press, 1997.

Ward, Wilfred. *The Life of John Henry Cardinal Newman Based on His Private Journals and Correspondence.* 2 vols. New York: Longmans Green, 1912.

———. *Last Lectures.* London: Longmans Green, 1918.

Whately, Richard. *Elements of Logic,* 9th ed. Boston: James Monroe and Co., 1858.

Wilken, Robert L. "Alexandria: A School for Training in Virtue." In *Schools of Thought in the Christian Tradition,* ed. Patrick Henry, 15–30. Philadelphia: Fortress Press, 1984.

Williams, Bernard. *Shame and Necessity.* Berkeley and Los Angeles: University of California Press, 1985.

———. *Ethics and the Limits of Philosophy.* Cambridge, MA: Harvard University Press, 1993.

———. *Truth and Truthfulness: An Essay in Genealogy.* Princeton, NJ: Princeton University Press, 2002.

Williams, Michael. *Problems of Knowledge: A Critical Introduction to Epistemology.* Oxford: Oxford University Press, 2001.

Wilson, Timothy D. *Strangers to Ourselves: Discovering the Adaptive Unconscious.* Cambridge, MA: The Belknap Press of Harvard University Press, 2002.

Wolterstorff, Nicholas. *John Locke and the Ethics of Belief.* Cambridge: Cambridge University Press, 1996.

Wynn, Mark. *Emotional Experience and Religious Understanding: Integrating Perception, Conception and Feeling.* Cambridge: Cambridge University Press, 2005.

Zagzebski, Linda T. *Virtues of the Mind: An Inquiry into the Nature of Virtue and the Ethical Foundations of Knowledge.* Cambridge: Cambridge University Press, 1996.

———. "Recovering Understanding." In *Knowledge, Truth, and Duty: Essays on Epistemic Justification, Responsibility, and Virtue,* ed. Matthias Steup, 235–251. Oxford: Oxford University Press, 2001.

Zahavi, Dan. *Subjectivity and Selfhood: Investigating the First-Person Perspective.* Cambridge, MA: MIT Press, 2005.

Index